La Famiglia Americana

T H E   A M E R I C A N   F A M I L Y

Fall 2002
" Piacere "

Paul Mugavero Baker

Printed and manufactured in
the United States of America

Cover Design, Story Editing & Book Composition by
Gary Adornato
Adeas Communications, Inc.
Baltimore, Maryland

Library of Congress Control Number: 2002095225

ISBN: 0-9661217-2-4

10 9 8 7 6 5 4 3 2 1

Dedication

To
Jacob McKenzie Baker,
Jacqlyn Olivia Baker, and
Austin Luis Baker,

The 5th Generation

Acknowledgements

First things first, I acknowledge my aunt, Anna Valianti Lolli whose poignant recall sparked my research and resolve. My other aunt, since deceased, Josephine Mugavero, supplied family history and Little Italy folklore. My father's vintage photos produced a visual theme. Joseph Luperini helped in translating the words, phrases and meanings, as well as supplying needed encouragement. On the west side of town Sam Prestianni did likewise.

My editor Gary Adornato again provided patience and understanding to the process. No commercial publisher would do what he deemed routine. He made the effort come alive and a dream come true.

Jack Gilden and his associate Evan Davis placed their agency, Gilden Integrated Advertising at our disposal to market the book. Account Executive Jay Schkloven coordinated their substantial effort.

Long time friend and respected *Sunpaper* drama critic emeritus, Lou Cedrone gave the work his candid benchmark and blessing. Friends and associates Vince Bagli, Ted Cox, Joe D'Adamo, Jack Degele, Tim Hodge, Jim Hodges, Jim Morgan, Steve Varanko and Brian Walsh provided marketing concepts and promotion avenues.

The following contributed pictures used in the book:

Bob Armstrong

Jeff Byron Photography

Lucille Cedrone

Dick Craig Photography

Paul Cummings

Ann D'Adamo

Ida DeFlavis

Joan Zimmerman Foit

John Geppi

Bill Hartleb

Vince Johns

Leo & Rob Maranto

Rudy Manelli

Maryland Historical Society

McKeldin Library, Univ. of MD

Mount St. Joseph's High School

Paulie Mugavero Collection

Johnny Pica, Jr.

Maria Pica

Brenda Simmons Rites

Frank Russo

Sun Source/The Sunpapers

Buck Ward

Author's Introduction

I was born in 1935 and grew up in West Baltimore during the end of the Depression and the beginning of the second World War. Italian on both sides, I was raised by my maternal grandparents who were born in Italy and spoke little English. My parents were first generation Americans who worked hard and sought upward mobility for themselves and their children – unlike their parents who were "Old World" entirely.

I thank my parents for nurturing me as an American. Despite their lack of formal education, they pointed me in the right direction and into a new modern world coming out of the Great War. They never spoke to me in Italian. Their outlook toward the times was; we are Americans, as good as the next person. They provided me with every opportunity at their disposal. Some which I took and others I rejected.

Books, magazines, newspapers and cultural opportunities made me think. And, having the name Baker kept me somewhat shielded from prejudice, which was still around into the 60's. They were not going to let their first born be a part of the "Mustache Pete" immigrant culture. I grew up as a "Joe College" in dress, attitude and overall outlook. I had a crew cut and short sideburns instead of the wavy pompadour. And yet, because of my grandparents and their ethnicity in a strange country, I was the recipient of their love, their humanity, and their culture. This work is an attempt to honor their memory. For them to come alive on these pages, no matter how fleeting, is reason enough to make the effort.

The stories and recollections should engender in the reader memories of your own upbringing. These stories are not woven into any kind of pattern that reaches a conclusion or gives a special message. They simply recall what it was like in those days, as remembered through the eyes of a young boy.

Preface

By the turn of the 20th Century Italians began to emigrate to America at an alarming rate of 200,000 plus per year. In 1925 there were 5,000,000 of them in the Continental United States. Most were dirt poor and illiterate contadino (the peasant class) from Southern Italy, an area composed of five provinces and the island of Sicily. The provinces are Abbruzzi, Campania, Apulia, Basilicata, and Calabria. Southern Italy is referred to as the "Mezzogiorno" – the land where time stood still. Being in the heart of the Mediterranean, over centuries the Mezzogiorno was inhabited, conquered and pillaged by dozens of tribes and nations. The most notable were the:

Austrians	Arabs	Byzantines
Carthaginians	French	Goths
Greeks	Normans	Phoenicians
Romans	Spanish	Vandals

Plus various Northern Italian powers and
wealthy feudal landowners.

As a result of centuries of turmoil, the foreigners left their culture, genealogy and social mores on the people of "the land where time stood still." The land was rocky and the heat unbearable. As the northern provinces began their move toward a unified Italy in the latter part of the 19th Century, the southern region was always neglected. To them the social reforms meant higher taxes and stiffer laws. The Mafia's appearance in Sicily can be directly traced back centuries to their opposition of oppression and conquest. Another byproduct of these centuries of turmoil was the formation of a close knit family structure that typifies Italians.

America was growing and her immigration laws were liberal. As conditions in Italy worsened from floods, earthquakes, volcanic eruptions, epidemics and political upheaval, the contadino let go of their homeland (La Miseria - Land of Misery) and the floodgates to America opened.

Settling mostly on the eastern seaboard, they stuck close together, trusted no one and worked hard at whatever menial jobs they could get. Theirs was the old way (la via vecchia), one where family came first and all other institutions were practically ignored. The Irish who had a fifty year head start were the police force of the nation, on the beat, in the churches, schools, the armed forces and, most importantly, in the job market. The first generation Italian father had no great love for the new land – a land that only transferred his squalor across the ocean. But, he persevered.

At home the Italian mother controlled the household. A bulwark of the family (la famiglia), she ran the gamut of job descriptions and human emotions. All the Italian songs about "mamma" are not without deep cultural meaning. La Famiglia included all the blood relatives, no matter how far removed, plus Godparents and very close friends, collectively called "compare." This amalgam of trust and love kept the immigrant Italians from despair. All first generation Italians clung to la via vecchia. First generation families thought nothing of keeping their offsprings out of school and in the job market, just like in the old country. Everyone bringing home a paycheck was of vital importance. Italians were grinders who made their living day by day. The Depression hardly made them blink. Statistics of the times showed that Italian school dropout rates were high, but they also were the lowest percentage of ethnics on welfare. Italians were and still are savers. Even today Italian families usually live below their means, an inherited trait from la via vecchia. As a result of centuries of oppression and their harsh entry into the new world, Italians can be described as wary, suspicious, guarded, stealthy and introverted.

The first generation made it hard on their children concerning old family traditions and the second generation found it just as hard to cross over and be American. Any move on their part was met with steely resentment. *"Chi lascia la via vecchia per la nuova sa quel che perde e non saquel che trova"* translates to, "Whoever gives up the old ways for the new, knows what he gives up, but not what he will find." This failure to assimilate kept Italian culture under wraps and, before the history could be properly chronicled, the era of mass media was upon us, producing a history of its own with the Untouchables, the Godfather series and now the Sopranos. They have stigmatized Italian culture in this country forever. But, America is so perverse that Italians are glamorized even when depicted as thugs. Nobel Peace Prize winners should get such notoriety.

Despite their efforts la via vecchia began to lose this war of attrition. Where 93% of first generation Italians married fellow Italians, the second generation slipped to 66%. By the third generation the meltdown was well underway. However, it was not until the end of World War II that the Italian colony in America truly became American. As far back as World War I (1914-1918), 400,000 first generation Italians fought for their new country. A quarter century later over 1.5 million Italian Americans served in World War II, representing over 10% of our fighting force. After World War II the second generation Italian American had options. He had an open invitation to join mainstream America. With the aging of the first generation, la via vecchia began to lose its powerful pull. The second generation began their Americanization full throttle.

The transplantation from Southern Italy to America has now taken root. We are who we are, not who we are perceived. Italians need no roll call of their famous citizens to claim legitimacy, nor the refutation of the Mafia to cleanse their souls. Italians made it on hard work and an unflinching honor to preserve the family values they hold so dear. Now in the 21st Century we are all Americans, as it should be.

The history lesson stops here. I am a product of second generation parents and was raised by my first generation grandparents. This work talks about people, places, and things that happened to me growing up as a third generation Italian American. I always avoided la via vecchia as a child. As a full blooded Italian, Abbrusezze/Siciliano, whose father Americanized his name, I wanted to be an American. Since then I have slowly begun to swing back to the other side. I have passed the traditions on to my fourth generation sons, who as children were nurtured by their second generation grandparents. This work is an effort to honor our past and give you the reader a chance to fill in your own blanks.

Now that the march from the boat is complete it is time to look back. There will be no more of:

> Grandpop Lolli's wine
> Adelina's sausage and macaroni from scratch
> Poppy's squeeze box
> DiNobili cheroots on a summer night
> Gigantic family dinners
> Latin masses
> Geppi's touchdown runs
> Men like Perry Como
> Men like Tommy D'Alesandro

But, as time slips by it should be comforting to the offspring of Italian immigrants that the time no longer stands still, and we have made it in America. La Famiglia still remains, if only in our hearts. I hope this book brings back your own happy memories of days gone by.

For best results, these stories should be read in a quiet place. Turn on instrumental Italian music, pour yourself a glass of wine and go with the flow.

Foreword

by Lou Cedrone, Jr.

Growing up Italian was a different experience for most of us who were sons of immigrants. The experience would change decade by decade, area by area.

Growing up Italian in the twenties and thirties differed from that same experience in the thirties and forties and differed again, from the experience in the forties and fifties.

Paul Baker's experience was in the thirties through the fifties when Italians had yet to become a part of the mainstream, a position they enjoy today.

It was World War II that made the difference. It was World War II that drew the dividing line, thanks, in part, to the participation of all those young Italian-Americans who served in the armed services and thanks, again, to the G.I. Bill, a piece of legislation that changed the face of America.

Baker's reminiscences take us back to West Baltimore of the thirties through the fifties; a time when uncles, aunts, cousins and paisons were a part of what was then the nuclear immigrant family.

The author's recall has a universal truth, at least to Italian-Americans. Baker's memories are warm and identifiable, but he doesn't limit his recall to the Italian-American citizens. His book, apart from the ethnic material, is also, in almost equal portion, a remembrance of characters the author knew, people who were part of his ken, his neighborhood.

In "La Famiglia Americana," he gives us a chance to acquaint ourselves with those people, to meet his relatives and to know the kind of world all Italian-Americans knew and enjoyed. We might not care to return to that world, but we wouldn't take a million for the memories.

Lou Cedrone, Jr. is a highly acclaimed former theater and drama critic for the Baltimore Sun (1951-1992). He is also a World War II veteran and the son of Louis Cedrone, Sr. – Poppy – as well as the uncle of Paul Baker's wife, Connie Peddicord Baker. An article featuring the Cedrone family begins on page 55.

Table of Contents

Section I

"La Famiglia"

The Family

La Famiglia
The Family

"Their marriage was arranged by family and friends. They settled down in Baltimore and raised nine children around the time of the Great Baltimore fire."

My father, a full-blooded Sicilian and the third of nine children, passed away on January 12, 1995. He was 85 and had been failing for several years. I had plenty of time to "close the book" with him. As my father faded away, I wanted to talk about our long relationship - all the whys and how comes - but we never got around to it. He was just my father. Explanations were wanted by me but not needed by him.

Born at 913 Fawn Street in the heart of Baltimore's Little Italy, Dad was christened Nicola Mugavero. His mother called him "Caulie," a derivative of Nicola. Tossed around the neighborhood, Caulie became Paulie. During the Roaring 20's and into the Depression when this full-blooded Sicilian became Paul Baker for reasons I never asked, my father worked odd jobs. He was an amateur boxer, a street hustler, a pool hall proprietor, and eventually helped manage the infamous Fiorita Club, a neighborhood speakeasy. When the Depression ended with the onset of World War II, my Dad began to move up in the world working as a surveyor's apprentice while getting his high school diploma at night from Baltimore Polytechnic. Recently married, he began to distance himself from his early life, the poor son of a

3

neighborhood bread maker named Gregorio. When working the streets of Little Italy Paulie was a slender, matinee idol type. But as a family man working a job in the Mutual Departments of the Maryland State Race Tracks, including Pimlico, and the ticket counter at Penn Station, he changed his persona forever.

With a fuller face and thick octagon bifocals, he transformed himself from pool room hustler to bookish ticket agent. It was a feat Robert DeNiro would have admired and one I neither understood nor had the courage to ask about.

His parents came over here "on the boat" separately. They were from the same area in Sicily but met in New York. Their mountain villages were Caltavuturo and Isnello, a few miles south of the beautiful fishing town called Cefalu.

Gregorio came over on a large steamer, The Giorgio, out of Naples. He arrived at Ellis Island on April 20, 1893. He was around 20-years old and lived in New York with relatives.

The Mugaveros: (left to right) Paulie Mugavero Baker, Connie Cherigo, Helen Motto, Rosie Mugavero, Mary Mugavero, Mamie Prouty, Josephine Mugavero, and Marion Mugavero. Circa 1975 at the Ronald Cherigo wedding... Paulie Mugavero collection

4

Salvatora arrived on a German vessel that sailed from Palermo, Sicily, arriving in New York on November 18, 1904. She also settled in New York with family and friends. Salvatora was 22 and unmarried.

Their marriage was arranged by family and friends. He was nine years older than his bride. They settled down in Baltimore and raised nine children around the time of the great Baltimore fire (1904). The children in order were, Concetina, David, Nicola (Paulie), Mamie, Rose, Josephine, Helen, Marion, and Mary. The house still stands mid-block between Sabatino's Restaurant and Mugaveros Confectionery store. The front had a bay window and double doors. Inside on the first floor were three large rooms, two in front and one in back. The second floor housed the large kitchen, a living room and a spacious parlor. On the third floor were four bedrooms. In the back of the kitchen was an open yard where Salvatora grew flowers, peppermint plants, and hung out the wash.

Gregorio's shop was on the first floor of the house. The floors were highly polished hickory wood. In the back rooms flour and brown sugar sacks were piled up to the ceiling. In the front room was the counter area. Every morning Gregorio would arise at 3:00 a.m. to knead the flour and bake the bread. The Mugavero Bakery thrived in the 1920's when the children were very young. Salvatora fashioned curtains for the store windows from the flour sacks. Washed, pleated and starched, they also were made into clothing for the children. As the Depression loomed immigrants used every-thing at their disposal to survive. The aroma from the mid-block bakery wafted over the entire street. Inside, the store was lit by gas lamps that were capped when not in use.

5

According to Josie, in 1927 the Mugaveros were the first family in Little Italy to have electricity. Gregorio made the coarse and crusty Sicilian loaves and thick squares of bread topped with tomatoes, cheese and anchovies. A Sicilian specialty.

Gregorio Mugavero

One frozen winter night, around 1930, tragedy struck. Davy, who was sleeping on the top of the flour sacks awakened to a shrill scream. His father's hand had been trapped in the mechanism of the new electric kneading machine. The family carried him through the streets up to Johns Hopkins Hospital on Broadway, a three mile trek through snow covered streets. There was no ambulance service at that time. Gregorio lost his right hand. Unable to work his trade, he took on small jobs as the Depression bore down on America.

Gregorio bought in bulk, storing cheese, pork and salami in the cool basement. He made wine every year, a red Marsalla. Salvatora made full, tasty meals from vegetables alone. She also made tuna fish salad from scratch. And, of course there was always bread and home made macaroni. "We were considered poor, but we always ate well. My father was a great provider," said Josie.

As the children grew older, to keep them from the public baths that pervaded the time, Gregorio fashioned a large tub from a discarded horse trough and made what today would be called a hot tub for his family.

I recall my grandfather as a quiet, somber man. He wore

a black, leather bow tie with a white shirt and a buttoned black vest. His injury was covered by a black stocking and he always had that arm folded under his other arm. He sat in a big chair and slept a lot. I never spoke to him but I always remember kissing him goodbye. I can still feel the stiff bristles of his mustache and the strength of his arms when he hugged me. He had velvet skin and I could tell he liked me. I was five and now, some sixty-plus years later, my Aunt Jo is reminded of her father whenever she sees me.

My grandmother was a different story. She always made a big fuss when we got up to the second floor kitchen. Salvatora was a typical Sicilian grandmother. She was around fifty years of age and wore thick glasses with her hair pulled back in a bun. I always tried to pull her glasses off much like my grandson, Jacob, now does to me. She dressed in standard Italian matron garb, a black dress with black stockings and bulky, thick-heeled black leather shoes. On occasion the black dress would have a print in it and sometimes she wore a sleeveless sweater. I was always met with a big "make over," hugs and wet smooches, then consternation and impatience, all during the same visit, and finally the big farewell. Even as a child I could feel her tension.

Of the six Mugavero girls only three married. The two oldest, Connie and Mamie married late in life and each had one child. Rosie and Mary passed away in 1981 and 1982. Neither married. Helen also married late at age 56. Josie, a stately and attractive matron describes the phenomenon thusly; their Sicilian mother who had been wed by the old fashioned process of arranged marriage was very strict with her girls. According to Josie the girls were confronted with "so many don'ts" that they were made to wonder "what were the do's." They did not have the mindset or parental consent to be courted. One night before the War started in earnest, Helen brought home a nice "American guy" for dinner. Everyone was cordial. There were no incidents, but everyone was aware of an "Americani" in the house. With Old World formal courting still being in vogue, the ethnic factor still loomed heavy. Mamie, a little older than Helen, married an American guy. Uncle Bill Prouty was a great fellow who "broke the line." It took Helen a longer time to find the man of her dreams, Sam Motto, who was from the neighborhood.

The Mugavero girls were always referred to by my mom and me as "The Aunts." Connie worked at the Poland and Katz Umbrella Company on Fayette Street and Park Avenue. Mamie, like my mother, worked in a sweat shop, the name given to the garment factories.

The youngest of the nine Mugavero children, Mary Mugavero was a tiny, energetic dynamo who set out early to

Rosie was a beautician who for many years ran her own beauty shop in the heart of East Baltimore at 1733 Gough Street. She developed a following and had hundreds of loyal customers. Helen had a great job at Lever Brothers. Josie was the manager and buyer for the Princess Shops in South Baltimore for over 40 years. *(Above, Rosie's business card.)*

Aunt Mary... Paulie Mugavero collection

seek the American Dream. She graduated with top grades from Seton High School and began a career at Glenn L. Martin's. During that period of great growth after the War Martins flourished and so did Aunt Mary. I was too young to know all the details of her life but what I will remember about her forever was her positive attitude and sunshine disposition. She always supported me in my interests. I got movie magazines from her and she took me to Baltimore Stadium in 1944 to see the Duke versus Navy football game, and eight years later when I was coming off that same field holding the game ball from St. Joe's 19-6 victory over Loyola, Aunt Mary was there with a hug and a proud smile. She loved golf, horseback riding, and the outdoors. She treated my three sons with the same warmth and encouragement she did me. God took her way too early. She typified to me, at an early age, that Italians were also Americans. A fact I never forgot. The Aunts always had a smile and an upbeat manner. They all loved me - I

"See You Later Charlie"

Charlie Kurtsinger was one of the nation's greatest riders and was War Admiral's jockey. Considered unbeatable, War Admiral raced the upstart Seabiscuit in a special "match race" at Pimlico. It was November 1, 1938.

On that day, the world literally stopped. Clem McCarthy's broadcast was heard by 40 million listeners including a totally absorbed FDR at his White House desk. Pimlico was packed with 40,000 fans as Grantland Rice described the scene; "keyed to the highest tension I have ever seen in sport." Seabiscuit (wearing blinders) pulled away in the stretch as jockey George Woolf coined the now famous phrase, "See you later Charlie."

could tell. All the hugs and pinches and folded dollars they slipped into my fingers every holiday.

Charlie Kurtsinger (head of table, right side) was a frequents visitor to the Fiorita Club, a Baltimore "speakeasy" run by Davy Mugavero Baker (far right).

The oldest boy, Davy, was the first to unofficially go by the name Baker. He was Davy, the Baker's boy. Around the time of the Depression he ran the famous Fiorita Club at 317 South High Street, one of the city's most "in" speakeasys. My father was his able assistant. They hosted celebrities and actors, the most prominent being the famous thespian, John Barrymore and Charlie Kurtsinger, world famous as War Admiral's jockey, was a frequent visitor. Davy died in 1937 of pneumonia.

Uncle Marion was a wild teenager who joined the Coast Guard and traveled all around the world...but you couldn't take Little Italy out of him. He has remained on "The Corner" fifty plus years and counting, running his store.

I was born in 1935, right after the Great Depression and just before World War II started. My parents lived with my maternal grandparents, Louis and Adelina Lolli, out in West Baltimore, a long way from Little Italy and its way of life. The Lolli's were from the province of Abruzzi on the Adriatic side of the Italian peninsula. Their towns were Teramo and Pescara. They were city people and a little better off than the Mugaveros.

Grandpop Lolli was a short, round guy who learned to cut hair and sew in an Italian orphanage. He had lots of friends from the "Old Country," several of whom he employed in his

A Lolli/Mugavero family gathering circa 1940
(left to right) Josephine Mugavero, Mary Lolli Mugavero Baker, "Sonny Baker", Mary Mugavero, Adelina Lolli, Salvatora Mugavero, Gregorio Mugavero, Luigi Manelli (compare), Louis Lolli, Bill Prouty, Mamie Mugavero Prouty, Connie Mugavero Cherigo, Charles Cherigo, Helen Mugavero, Marion Mugavero, and Rosie Mugavero. Note: Luigi Manelli and Luigi Lolli with napkins on their heads to absorb perspiration. There was no air conditioning. (Missing: Dave Mugavero deceased and Paulie Mugavero who was the photographer.). . . Paulie Mugavero collection.

tailor shop in Union Bridge, Maryland. He was always smoking those smelly, crooked De Nobili cheroots and drinking his home-made wine.

My grandmother Adelina raised me from birth until I became a teenager. She too wore the Old World garb. Her peasant upbringing was masked by her ethnicity. She was a force in the household and my Sergeant-at-Arms. Both my parents worked late as did Grandpop Lolli. So, for over a decade it was just me and Adelina.

Eighteen North Hilton Street was in a working class West Baltimore neighborhood on the cutting edge of suburbia. We were surrounded by Americani. Anyone who was not Italian was Americani. There was no animosity, no prejudice or hard

11

feelings, but most Italians thought their way of life was best. After all, Adelina had a Bread Man, an Oil Man, an Ice Man, a Fruit and Vegetable Man, and a Fish Man. We even had a knife sharpener who came into our backyard. There were many peddlers coming through our neighborhood. We knew them all. Americans went to stores for their food.

Our row house was on the corner and got lots of sun. We led the neighborhood in awnings. Front porch, side porch, back porch and all the windows were under green-striped, canvas awnings. Our small front lawn was so overgrown with bushes, plants and flowers, I called it the Garden of Eden. On the side of the house, surrounded by a concrete border was our beloved fig tree. In winter it was wrapped in Grandpop's armhole bastings to protect it from the frost. In the back of the house was a solid brick, two-car garage. Our front porch and steps were poured concrete making it cool in summer and frigid in winter. Like most Italians we lived in the basement which housed an oil-burning furnace, a wine cellar, a washtub area, and a dank, dark pantry. The center of the basement was the kitchen. I could never understand that upstairs, was a fully equipped, modern American kitchen that just sat there for years unused like a show room floor model. Also on the first floor was our parlor (living room) with an adjoining formal dining room. Whenever company came we used these rooms. Upstairs were four decent sized bedrooms with a square hallway in the center. We only had one bathroom and that became a problem at times. Later on I came to find out that Luigi and Adelina had a chamber pot under their bed for emergency use, a vestige of the old country. Overall, it was a nice house. I always had my own bedroom and never had to share space like so many ethnic kids.

The Italian network did extend out from Little Italy. Two days a week we got fresh Italian bread from Maranto's, the conventional loaves on Tuesdays and Sicilian on Thursdays.

My first Holy Communion... a poster boy for Italia... Paulie Mugavero collection

And the neighborhood grocery store did stock Luigi's De Nobilis in plastic six packs. Victor Broccolino would come periodically to sell, repair, and clean watches and jewelry. Italians treasured the keepsakes of the Old Country. Through our back alley came hucksters and street A-rabs walking their pony-drawn fruit and vegetable carts. Redneck, hillbilly types, they did stock items for the "signoras" of the neighborhood. Peering out the back bedroom window into the alley below, I would watch Adelina bargaining with the A-rab over peppers, artichokes, egg plant and fruits. Pigeon English and Abruzzesse haggling in a West Baltimore alley on a muggy summer morning, priceless.

For the most part we were displaced Italians, living out of familial enclaves. Living among Americans. Any religious, social, or family gatherings were still Little Italy based. These people were not ready to become Americans. What was I to do? Where did I fit in?

Paulie Mugavero

"I have concluded that my father wanted to be an American — not an Italian-American or an American-Italian — all the while, never being ashamed of his heritage."

The Mugavero family was proud and industrious. Everyone pitched in. But, before the children were old enough to lend support, things got rough as the Great Depression was just around the corner. Paulie Mugavero never went to high school. He worked the streets to make ends meet. He ran a small pool room and sold hot dogs and sodas. At the end of the Roaring 20's, he was just turning 20. It was a hard time for Italian males. The huge wave of immigration from southern Italy in the first quarter of the 20th Century dumped several million uneducated, swarthy, Italians onto our shores. All they needed was $25 for passage and $20 to show at Ellis Island and they were good to go. Out of their own enclaves, they were persona non-grata.

Was it wrong for my father to distance himself from this rabble? In terms of self preservation alone, I think not. When he was 18 years old, the famous Sacco-Vanzetti case cast a dark shadow on young Italian males. Around this time my father became involved in the "Fiorita Club" at 317 South High Street in Little Italy. It was a famous after-hours place right around the time of the Depression. He also changed his

Paulie, in passenger seat, with his "speakeasy boys," in Patterson Park. Circa 1930... Paulie Mugavero collection

name to the trade of his father and became Paul Baker. Many Italians changed their names for a variety of reasons during these times, including his best friend Vince Lazzara who became Vince Dundee of boxing fame. So, when my father met his wife to be, he was Paul Baker. I do know that during my lifetime with him, my father never said or did anything to lead me to believe he was ashamed of being Italian. But, he never publicized it and preferred to be known as an American.

He seemed more intelligent than the average immigrant's son and knew early on that he had to get out of Little Italy and become an American, the sooner the better. Although he was Italian through and through, he was not hung up with an "Old World" mentality. He struggled all during his teen years and into his 20's. When he married Mary Lolli, from West Baltimore, he started to find legitimate work and put Little Italy in his rear view mirror, permanently. Other than his kid brother, Marion, who stayed in Little Italy his

The Sacco-Vanzetti Case

Two young Italian men, Nicola Sacco and Bartolomeo Vanzetti were arrested and accused of murdering a shoe factory paymaster and his guard on April 15, 1920.

The evidence convicting them was circumstantial. After six years of appeals and public protests, they could not overturn the original verdict. The negative attitude towards Italians seemed to seal their doom.

Both men were executed on August 23, 1927. At the time my father was 17-years old and working in a speakeasy.

The young Paulie Mugavero, who worked the streets of Little Italy, had all the dashing good looks of a matinee idol type guy... Paulie Mugavero collection

Barely Amici

In the Italian pecking order, first and foremost, was La Famiglia, consisting of all blood relatives no matter how far removed and 'Compare, meaning God Parents and very close friends. Casual friends without deep ties were called amici. As Paulie lived with his in-laws, a steady stream of Luigi and Adelina's 'Compare traipsed through the house, barely amici to him. Think about it.

entire life, all of the Mugaveros overlooked his "disgracia" and still loved him dearly. After he got married, his luck changed and he was hired by the Maryland Pari-Mutual Department as a cashier at the State's race tracks. And, then by the Pennsylvania Railroad as a ticket clerk. He ended up working these jobs religiously for over 40 years.

My father was an accomplished pen and ink sketch artist who had a chance to work for a fledgling outfit in California named Walt Disney Enterprises. Also, in the early 40's Vince Dundee offered him a partnership to run his restaurant. But the legit, sure thing that he had worked so hard to attain was where he stayed. His crazy work schedule made our relationship a tenuous one. He lived his entire married life in the home of his in-laws. He was an intractable Sicilian seeking upward mobility in America, under the same roof with two Italian-born immigrants from Abruzzi, who couldn't speak English and could not understand the Sicilian dialect. No wonder he worked 60-hours a week.

My father took me to major league baseball games at Griffith Stadium in Washington, D.C. plus Redskins and Navy football games in Baltimore. More importantly, he made me aware of history. He and my mother would take turns reading me American History before bedtime. *Life Magazine* and *Reader's Digest* plus *The Baltimore Sun* and *Baltimore News-Post* were in the home. He introduced me to classical music and opera at an early age. On his rare off-days we would take advantage of his railroad passes and take the train to New York for a play or a game. Invariably, we would stop at a famous restaurant. I remember Luchow's, Jack Dempsey's and some fancy art galleries. We visited Fort McHenry, the Pratt Library, and all the art galleries of Baltimore. All these experiences helped form my persona. Eventually, I was the first person in our family to graduate from college and I became a History teacher.

I have concluded that my father wanted to be an American – not an Italian-American or an American-Italian – all the while, never being ashamed of his heritage. But you still couldn't take the Sicilian out of him. He was always nervous and jumpy. It was as if he wanted anonymity for himself and his family. He seemed to worry that some unknown force might suddenly appear and deposit him back to Little Italy and poverty. He was big on American History and respect for authority.

We clashed from the first day I can remember. Over anything and everything. He couldn't get past his old-fashioned Sicilian upbringing. My father was always critical and suspicious. On our many trips he would go off hard on me if I ever talked to strangers at a baseball game or in public places. To Sicilians, everyone was a stranger – someone to be reckoned with. In the meantime, I was spoiled by everyone, especially my mother, the aunts and Grandma Lolli. My father didn't know what to make of me. We were both stubborn people. My sister Jeannette came 10 years after me, so as I entered my teen years he began to concentrate on her. He did a remarkably better parenting job the second time around from the simple standpoint of "lightening up."

Because of his work schedule my father was not involved in the daily responsibilities of raising his son. He never showed me much emotion. His father had a tough life raising nine children and I think that reflected on his relationship with me. Love and affection would come from my mother. She would take me to work with her on Saturdays. I think she was proud of her first born and enjoyed "showing me off" to her many ethnic friends. I can still feel the rat-a-tat-tat vibrations of those sweat shop sewing machines and the hot steam flowing upwards from the giant pressers. I would lay in a bed of basted garments, eating candy and watching my mom sew and chatter. (My father forbade me to eat candy. He would smell my breath and check my pockets.) The sweat shop was filled with smiling immigrants happy to be working. At noon we would leave, going uptown to lunch at Reads Pharmacy. Then, a movie at the Century or Keith's on Lexington Street, followed by a shopping spree. It was a happy time. Children of the Depression, my parents gave me all the things they never had. They were the unpolished Yuppies of their time, making up for the lost years as children of immigrants.

In attempting to understand my father and what made him tick, I must look at history. Southern Italians who flocked to America by the millions in the decades between 1880 and World War I were poor, uneducated and totally unfit for assimilation into American life. These people clustered together in eastern cities forming hundreds of areas similar to our Little Italy. Driven from their homeland by force and coercion they made the trip over with great trepidation. For many it was a last resort, for others it was a new beginning.

These first generation immigrants developed a system of attitudes, values and customs that allowed them to live within themselves and unto themselves. No matter the degree or style of oppression, they brought with them a psychological stability and sense of security. The price was isolation from the American mainstream.

The immigrant's children, the "second generation" faced more complex challenges. They could not maintain the strident attitude of their old world parents. They had to cope with American institutions. What worked for their parents became a conflict for them. Part of the second generation compromise was the rejection of the "old ways." They resisted learning the Italian culture and language and thus became ill-equipped to teach it to the third generation.

Small numbers of the second generation carried the conflict to extreme. Separating from the clan they became enmeshed in American ways, giving their time and energy to schools, companies and organizations. The price they paid for siding with American culture was a strong sense of guilt and constant identity crisis, not quite compensated by their middle class position in American society. The compromise of the second generation Italian left him permanently in the lower middle class of America. Their children, the third generation, are still confused about their heritage. Yearning to be Americans, but clinging to the last vestiges of their ethnicity.

Paul Mugavero Baker

Paulie Mugavero's grandsons. (from left) Steve Baker, Nick Baker and Greg Baker.

21

could be Exhibit A. He left his first generation heritage behind quickly and early, then spent decades looking back and wondering, all the while living with the name Baker, a vanilla Anglo name, when actually he was "Caulie Mugavero, the Baker's boy." His third generation son, me, was just as confused. Wondering whether to let the Italian come in or leave it behind forever.

I lived under the roof of my first generation grandparents in a home reflecting everything Italian. Food, customs, religion, relationships all had Old World connotations. My parents worked long hours and became Americanized quick-ly. Our home was disjointed but not dysfunctional. The clashing between my parents and grandparents was real. There I was in the middle of this "opera" basically on my own. One foot in each world. I had a lot of freedom, except for certain "command performances" like church and Sunday dinner. I ignored my grandparents, especially as I grew older, and my parents' schedules precluded their influence, so I took orders from no one. This is a trait that has plagued me my entire life. Their only element of control was a refusal to let me drive.

Never having been in the service and never working a traditional nine to five regimen, rules and regulations always escaped me. Perhaps that explains the fact that I attended so many different high schools and colleges and having no deep rooted allegiance to any of them. This behavior was acquired but its genesis is Italian. Sicilian to be exact.

I did help raise three fourth generation sons who grew up with no "old world" hang-ups, but all the while enjoying their second generation Grand Parents with unconditional love.

My father was self-educated and hungry for knowledge.

In his own way he provided me with the atmosphere and the thirst for the good life. For a guy from humble, impoverished roots he did a pretty good job. Also, he was a good and unselfish provider. He disappeared into the fabric of America, never to emerge. So eager to escape from being a "Depression Hooligan" he became an American, totally and completely. Forty years of working on the railroad, literally and figuratively. Growing up all I ever did was try to "play ball." My father rarely came to see me play. When I became a high school and college coach, he rarely came to see a game. To me he was not the Paulie Mugavero depicted on page 17 of this book. My whole life I had to scramble. He wanted me to be more stable, more American. I guess he, more than anyone, saw the Italian that was deeply inside me.

My father's only hobby was photography. He took pictures of everyone in the family. His camera was omnipresent, yet he never taught me to take pictures or allowed me to touch his cameras. So much for the saying, "teach someone to fish and they will never go hungry." But, many of the pictures in this book now live from Paulie Mugavero's collection. And, it is heartening to see his grand-son, Nick, running all over Chuck E. Cheese snapping pictures and filming his daughter Jackie's first birthday party. Dad would have been proud.

When you look back to the Mugaveros of Fawn Street a few years after the Great Fire, then the Roaring 20's and the Great Depression, the strength of the family and Sicilian roots have served us all well. I miss my father now, having left many things unsaid. But his artifacts are all around me and, when I walk through parts of our town, like the Main Pratt Library, St. Leo's Church and the site of Memorial

Stadium, I feel him. When I hug my fourth generation, blue-eyed, one-quarter Italian grandson Jacob, knowing that my blood and my father's blood is in him, I cannot ask for more.

Mom

"Lack of formal education notwithstanding, Mom was well spoken, well dressed, and possessed a presence that exuded class."

Mary Lolli was born in a row house on Conway Street near the present day site of Camden Yards. It was 1914. Her two brothers Arnoldo and Nicola were still stranded in Italy. Luigi and Adelina would move two more times, to a small farm off West Baltimore Street and, eventually, to 18 North Hilton Street. Mary never went past the fourth grade, working around the house and in her father's tailor shop. She was great with a needle and thread.

Only Italian was spoken in the home, but miraculously Mom, who spoke and understood Italian fluently, had no hint or inflection of the Italian tongue. It was as if the process went through her, leaving no tell tale signs. This miracle permeated her entire persona. She was American through and through in her dress, mannerisms and the aforementioned language. In this respect she and Paulie Mugavero were kindred spirits.

Mom was a brilliant seamstress. Above, my sister Jeannette models a prize winning "smocked dress," made by Mom, at the State Fair in Timonium in September, 1950... Paulie Mugavero collection

25

Mom, on vacation in Florida and "dressed for the occasion."
Spring, 1944... Paulie Mugavero collection

Many a time I would hear my mother in full blown Abbrusezze dialect with Adelina, then turning to me with a grammatically perfect English enunciation, all in the same breath. No one was to talk to Sonny in Italian. Mom and Dad were the post Depression Era yuppies who wanted a better life for themselves and their families. My mother worked full time in Baltimore's tailor shops, aptly called "sweat shops," from the time I was born til the mid seventies. And after that, part time. A half century of tedium motivated by the hard times.

Mary Lolli Mugavero Baker never lost her capacity for hard work. She spoiled me, giving me all the things she never had. Lack of formal education notwithstanding, Mom was well spoken, well dressed, and possessed a presence that exuded class. Whenever she was in over her head, her smile and demeanor kept her in the game. She wanted the best for her two children. Her three grandchildren loved her

The wedding portrait of Paulie and Mary in 1934.
Best man is Nicky Lolli and Maid of Honor is Rosie Mugavero

27

dearly and I feel their relationship was very rewarding to her. When the boys would call her "Granny" and mimic her commands, she would light up.

In the eighties, when I was in sales, I would stop over to see Mom every week. We would sit in the kitchen, just the two of us, and talk. She wanted to know about me and my life and my family.

Being Depression Era second generation Italians, my parents always worried about "how we were doing." College educated (through their finances and encouragement), I never became a doctor, lawyer, executive, or well to do business man. But Mom and Dad, because of you and what you sacrificed, all is well in our family.

Grandpop Lolli

(Arnoldo and Mary's Father)

"Luigi loved to drink home made Italian wine and smoke those crooked Di Nobili cheroots."

On September 2, 1951, at the age of 63, Louis Lolli died of a massive heart attack. He collapsed at the dinner table on a Sunday afternoon. Originally he and Adelina bought a small farm in Southwest Baltimore. Early in the Depression they had to sell the farm and moved a few miles up the road to Hilton Street in the St. Joseph's Monastery parish. Luigi went to work for some of the top clothiers in town as a designer of men's clothing. Eddie Jacobs, Grue, and Solomon vied for his services. Their daughter, Mary, my mom, grew up in a tailor shop. Right before the Depression Luigi and Adelina sent for their other two children, Arnoldo and Nicola, who had been left in Italy with relatives because of the impending War and their own uncertainty with life in the new world.

Luigi loved to drink homemade Italian wine and smoke those crooked Di Nobili cheroots. On a summer night he would sit on the front porch in his undershirt enjoying the remains of the day. He worked six days a week. Sunday was for the family. He would take me to church in his little yellow roadster convertible. When we got back, the dinner was on the table.

In the early forties, he worked at Fort Meade and the Naval Academy, making clothes for the servicemen of World War II. Every Christmas and Easter he would "measure me up" with chalk, pins and tape and produce a tailor-made outfit. Just what a 10-year-old Italian kid needed. It might have been easier to paint a bullseye on my back and chest. Ironically, since his passing I have never owned a tailor-made suit. On occasion he would take me to the tailor shop. And there, among all these Americani, Grandpop Lolli would

Grandpop Lolli with his ever present Di Nobili cigar.

hold court. With a tape measure around his neck, loosened silk tie, and buttoned vest, he would begin his design making notes and chalking up the dummy model. All eyes were transfixed on this little rolly-poly Italian man with the ever present Di Nobili in the side of his mouth. They followed his every move and gesture with knowing respect. Grandpop Lolli spoke to the occasion using his "best" broken English. It was a sight I will always remember, as cultures crossed into one. It's called Americanization. His gift to me.

Adelina

"For the most part, everyone in the neighborhood liked Mrs. Lolli. It was a time in our history that the tide in the world was turning and everyone, regardless of origin, was pulling together."

What a piece of work. Italian, head to toe, trapped in America. Built like a block of granite, she transcended age and gender. Adelina would cook all day and at dinner time there was food for an army. As a young child I was tied to her apron strings. I watched her cook, went along to the markets, and sat in Mrs. Bossi's kitchen while she visited over coffee and cake. She seldom spoke to Americani on the street other than an expressive nod as she maintained the right-of-way.

Adelina always went to church. It was her connection to the Old Country while living on foreign soil. The Latin Mass and pageantry at St. Joseph's Monastery were right up her alley. The Passionist Fathers from Union City, New Jersey who traveled the world as missionaries for Christ were her favorites. The small Italian representation was buoyed by the presence of Father Adrion Poletti (dead ringer for today's movie star, Paul Sorvino) and Father Albert Catanzaro. Religion was the magic elixir for the Italian immigrants. Adelina was very proud when I became an Altar Boy.

Always feeling out of place in American neighborhoods, Italians could rally around in a Catholic church.   The

31

language, which embarrassed me on the streets when spoken by Adelina and her cronies, was exalted inside the church where strains of Ave Maria and Panis Angelicus were bouncing off the walls. For those brief moments, all of a sudden it was our world.

Her house was an open door for fellow paisanos. Adelina always had coffee, vino and cookies available. As a result, there was a passing parade of immigrant types traipsing through our house, patting me on the head on their way to the "dago red" and other delights in Adelina's basement kitchen. My father, a guest in the home of his in-laws and an ultra conservative, was taken aback big time by the flavor of this household, which was sort of an Italian halfway house. The hard core first generation Italians would usually enter quietly through the cellar door. Dad and Adelina had a tenuous relationship best described as a "permanent truce." One Machiavelli would have crafted.

Paul was a proud Sicilian with seemingly no future, working in pool parlors and speakeasies, trying to get enough money to buy Mary Lolli a ring. Adelina and Luigi, both from Abruzzi, had a little cash, a home, and gainful employment. In his favor, Paul was Italian, handsome, and from a good family. When Adelina saw Gregorio, Salvatora and the Mugavero clan, she caved in, consented and opened up her home. But after the honeymoon, "the truce," with all it's ramifications, took over. Adelina loved cats. Paul hated cats. Adelina loved people and noise. He was reclusive. Adelina had Old World hygiene habits. Paul was meticulous with movie star teeth. His weekly Life magazines and Baltimore newspapers, constantly underfoot, were a big bone of contention. Paul was always squirreling away his periodicals from the clutches of Adelina, who couldn't read and could care less. On Saturdays, the Metropolitan Opera was on the air, loud. I can never recall my father and Adelina having a lucid conversation.

Our next door neighbors were the Fountains, austere Methodists with country roots. How they withstood the noise, broken English, and the Old World garlic and onion smells, I never knew. But there was never a harsh word or any outward animosity. Except one day when I clubbed their son Ferdie over the head with a pipe. Adelina whipped me hard, then sent food over the back fence for a week.

For the most part, everyone in the neighborhood liked

"Mrs. Lolli." It was a time in our history that the tide in the world was turning and everyone, regardless of origin, was pulling together.

Once a week, Adelina dragged me along to the market. Most of the Italian stores were downtown and Adelina had a circuit she traveled from Baltimore and Hilton streets to Lexington Market and back. Lexington Market was close to

Adelina shepherding over her two prized possessions, grandchildren "Sonny Baker" (left) and "Louie" Lolli (Arnoldo's son). Circa 1939... Paulie Mugavero collection

St. John's Church where we occasionally stopped in to light a candle. As a pre-schooler I remembered the smells of stale cheese, garlic, herbs and live chickens. There were no supermarkets. Just some grocery stores with American food. We would go at midmorning after the work traffic subsided and the trolleys weren't crowded. She had on her usual outfit. If it was cool, she carried a wool shawl, black of course. Adelina was in her early fifties. She was hefty and strong. Probably 5'2", around a buck eighty. She had just a few teeth and a large mole on her cheek. She spoke no English and was quite loud. Wherever we went she got a wide berth. At the market she knew lots of the vendors and, when she stormed into Trinacria's Italian Grocery Store on Paca Street, they practically stood at attention. In those days these stores didn't deliver, so Adelina was selective on her trips. The worst days were when she bought the smelly fish called "baccalla" (cod in a smelly "powder"). No matter how well the grocer wrapped it, the trolley ride home was a killer.

But the coup de grace were the days she would buy the live chicken. Striding through the pens, peering for the plumpest birds, she would spot her prey. The little Italian clerk would reach into the wooden pen and grab the flapping, smelly thing by the legs, bind it with cord, stuff it into Adelina's double shopping bag, and away we would go. All the way home, the chicken would be struggling to get free, flapping and cackling. As the trolley began to fill up, she would holler for the

Sicilian Icon

Trinacria still stands. Over 102 years old, this Sicilian Temple is one of the oldest stores in Baltimore. Along with the St. Jude Shrine down the street, it is a slice of Italian folklore spanning two centuries. *Trinacria* translates into "island of the triangle" – Sicily.

chicken to behave, like it was a human being, in Italian, of course. I was only five, but I was sure as hell embarrassed.

Sometimes, on our way home, we would hit Hollins Market and then the homes of several or so first generation Italian immigrants living along this route. These Italian houses looked, smelled and seemed identical. Statues and holy pictures were omnipresent.

Adelina and I sharing a special moment one Christmas... Paulie Mugavero collection

There was Jesus pointing to his bleeding heart, a crucifix on the wall, and some serious looking people with halos behind their heads. There were rosaries and candles seemingly in every room. Downstairs were wine cellars with herbs, garlic, onions and peppers hanging from the ceiling. Outside in the yard were peppermint plants, a fig tree and a full fledged vegetable and flower garden. Because the husbands and growing offsprings were out making a living, these gardens were functional but not well groomed. There was a wash board, clothes line, clothespins and a huge wash tub. All the houses on her "circuit" were so similar that when friends ask me if I have ever been to Italy, my reply is always the same. I nod and smile, "many times."

On these social visits, I was showered with mushy kisses and garlic hugs, then put in a corner while the two gals visited. They always drank that bad-smelling coffee and chattered in their native dialect. The inflections were loud and fractured. I never understood a word but I knew when they lowered their octave it was something spicy. I have an Italian friend from Syracuse who does the same thing to me today whenever he unloads a secret thought. There was no TV to divert the waiting and when Adelina loosened up her brogans, I knew we were in for a long stay. Her right leg would always swell up badly. She broke it in the Spring of 1936 carrying me into the house. I could always tell that they were having a great time so I tried to be patient. And, they always gave me candy. In all my years growing up I never remember Adelina having a prolonged conversation with anyone but an Italian person.

When we got home, the fun started. I viewed this horrific scene only once, but it left an indelible impression on me. In the silence of our basement kitchen, she snapped the chicken's neck, took out a cleaver and chopped its head off, placing the severed neck over the front burner, all in the blink of an eye. She then cut off the legs and began to pluck all the feathers off. Then the naked corpse was washed off and soaked in a large pot. Later, she took the cleaver, opened up the bird, pulling out the good stuff and throwing out the insides. She was doing what she had seen her mother do, and probably her mother's mother. To this day, I try to avoid eating chicken in any way, shape or form.

Adelina was there for my Holy Communion, Confirmation, and graduations. Not everyone had a grandmother like Adelina, but from parochial school, through high school and college, I never got to spend any meaningful time with her. We had a language barrier, an age difference and a huge cultural gulf. I was heading as far away from her generation and my roots as teenage legs could carry me. Yet, we had a bond that was genuine. She was always there for me, regardless. In another time and place I know we would have been great friends. She died just a few months before I got married. But she did meet my wife and gave her nod of approval. So I guess it's safe to say that I always had a woman in my life. There are so many things I would like to tell her and so many questions to ask.

A youthful Adelina and Luigi make a striking couple in this photo from the Old World.

Arnoldo

"At Christmas time Arnoldo would sell Christmas trees on the lawn in front of his shop. According to his son Lou, invariably he gave away half the trees to friends and customers who needed a boost. He was always about giving."

When Grandpop Lolli and Adelina came to America just before World War I, they left their oldest child, Arnoldo, and his little brother Nicola back in Italy. They planned to bring them over after "things got settled." Because of their adjustment to America and the beginning of the War the boys remained in Italy longer than planned. They stayed with their grandmother, whose name was Cantoressi, but were educated in the local orphanage in Teramo where Arnoldo learned to cut hair and play the saxophone.

The Lolli's daughter, my mother, Mary, was born in Baltimore in 1914. When they finally met, Arnoldo was 20 and Mary was 15. He was not too thrilled about coming over after being neglected for so long.

Nicola (left) and Arnoldo waiting in Italy for "the word." Circa 1926.

39

Genesis

Throughout the early 20th Century poor boys were educated at local Italian orphanages in their native land, where they learned a trade and to play a musical instrument. It was no coincidence that Italian immigrants cut hair or played in a band. With a comb and scissors or a horn, thousands of young Italians made it American.

He had established his own persona and social life in Italy.

Nicola Lolli had a short life. He died of kidney failure at the age of 20.

Grandpop Lolli had established his own tailor shop in Union Bridge, Maryland and employed many fellow immigrants. Arnoldo worked in the shop but was preoccupied with chasing the female employees. Grandpop Lolli sent him packing. Arnoldo would become a barber.

In nearby Westminster, the Grué family was also in the tailoring business. Through the Grués, Arnoldo met the Valianti family and fell in love with their oldest daughter Anna

Lolli's Union Bridge, MD tailor shop, circa 1925. Luigi (with neck tie) and his immigrant workers.

40

who was 17. She viewed Arnoldo, then 23, as an old man, a greenhorn from the other side. But he persisted. Every Sunday he would visit, bringing buns and bread up from Baltimore, first bonding with Mr. and Mrs. Valianti, cutting everyone's hair, all the while eyeing Anna. He was lonesome and unfulfilled looking for the good life but still pining for his native land. All native born Italians seemed to be "on loan" to America. On one occasion Arnoldo told Papa Valianti what started out to be a funny story. While waiting for his parents to "reclaim" him, Arnoldo would pack his guitar and a little suitcase to go on weekend sojourns through the Italian countryside, seeking and usually finding wine, women and song. The Lollis were from Abruzzi and the Valiantis from the nearby province of The Marches. Arnoldo told the story of "cocha bianco" (the white-headed one), an old lady who sold hot chestnuts outside the army barracks in the town of Ascoli Piceno. It was the late 20's. Papa Valianti listened intently as Arnoldo continued about the old lady. In addition to selling the chestnuts, she would engage the soldiers in a card game, which she always won. The soldiers would scurry to the cart of "cocha bianco" every payday to try their luck, but as the saying goes, she seemed to be able to "see through the cards." As Arnoldo continued to speak of the old lady Papa Valianti began to weep. "Cocha bianco" was his mother, whom he had not seen for over 20 years. A bond was formed.

As far back as the 20's, Italians were persona non grata everywhere. Papa Valianti took his family to Westminster from Belnord Avenue in East Baltimore. Living in the "campagna" and working in the tailoring business would be a nice life, but it was not an easy transition. There were already clusters of Sicilian immigrants there, many of whom were bootleggers who had provoked the ire of the townspeople. Papa Valianti left his barrel of home-made wine behind and settled in, but the children were targets of scorn. Anna recalls the name-calling and stone throwing. As a result the brothers Americanized their names. Romeo became Raymond, Dino became Daniel, Guarino became Reno, and Luigi became Louis. These were not easy times for Italians.

Finally, after two years of courting the timing was right and Arnoldo won his prize. Anna was 19 and just about finished raising all of her brothers and sisters. She had gone through two years of high school. Anna Valianti was ready to get her life started. Arnoldo was her one and only boyfriend. They were married in a formal wedding service at St. John's Church in Westminster. The wedding had been postponed for one year out of respect and mourning for Nicky's untimely death. It was 1935, the year I was born.

One night during the courtship, Arnoldo took Anna for a spin in Grandpop Lolli's yellow roadster, through the Westminster countryside. Upon reaching a lover's lane - alone at last thought Arnoldo. Suddenly, from the rumble seat pops Anna's precocious little brother, Raymond Valianti, to disrupt the moment. This would not be Romeo's last illicit escapade as he became the unofficial Baltimore Colt gadfly/ mascot when they trained in his native Westminster, during the

The Name Game

As we move into the 21st century it is not hard to understand that names like Hollis, Lacy, Dillon, Jacob McKenzie, Heather and Tanner belong to great, great grandchildren of hard core, first and second generation Italians.

42

50's. He became known as the guy who got caught bringing up beer and shrimp to Johnny Unitas and his pals in the Western Maryland College dorms after midnight.

The newlyweds moved to Baltimore. The Depression was just ending, but times were hard. Arnoldo held various jobs, selling oil burners and also trying real estate. Finally, he settled in as a barber, working in a huge shop on Greenmount Avenue. Anna taught Arnoldo, who was hardly able to speak the language, basic English words such as

Arnoldo and Anna's wedding portrait taken at St. John's Church in Westminster, MD in 1935.

"haircut" and "shave." In the meantime, she and her sister-in-law, Mary Lolli, worked in the Joseph Bank tailor shops, doing piece work at 1.5¢ per buttonhole. After becoming pregnant they worked at home. The truck would deposit stacks of goods early in the morning and pick them up at night. Anna and Mary would literally be "sewing in their sleep" as they relentlessly worked through the day to finish the pile of garments. My father worked for the City of Baltimore in a surveyor's crew and went to Poly night school. He eventually caught on with the Pennsylvania Railroad as a ticket clerk and worked seasonally in the Pari-Mutual Department of the Maryland State Race Tracks. Italians worked hard to make it in this country. As a child, every morning when I awakened, I found the house empty, except for Adelina, who was in the cellar cooking peppers and eggs for us and any down and out stragglers who might pop in. Grandpop Lolli and my parents were long gone, off to work. Some days my father was asleep behind a closed door, waking up at mid-day to go to his second job.

Arnoldo and Anna bought a house in West Baltimore, just a block or so from his parents, who lived at 18 North Hilton Street. Hilton intersected with West Baltimore Street. Hilton Street signaled the end of the line for Baltimore Street, that ran all the way back through downtown Baltimore, past Patterson Park, to its end at Haven Street. Baltimore Street was the defining East-West thread across our city up through the 60's. Their house was at #2 Abingdon Avenue, the last side street to intersect Baltimore Street. They paid a high price of $3,950 for the end of a row. Arnoldo put his barber shop in the basement and Anna began to raise a family. Louie, Dolores and Vince were born in 1937, 1939, and 1945.

A little guy with a quick, nervous gait and a pencil thin moustache, Arnoldo was a skilled old fashioned scissor barber, who drank black coffee and dangled a Lucky Strike precariously from his lip. As a teenager I was very much into the "flat-top whiffle cut" that all the ballplayers sported. I went to Gil Bateman's barber shop on Phelps Lane off Hilton Street for my cut, much to the chagrin of my family, especially my father who came down hard on me for my disloyalty. But Uncle Arnold always remained cool about it and never held it against me. We had our own thing. We would always talk baseball and boxing. He had enough customers anyway. Everybody knew "Lolli," "Lolli, the barber". He was one of the few "born on the other side" people who had dialogue and interaction with Americani.

Even though he was a greenhorn immigrant, everyone loved Uncle Arnold. The Americani called him Lolli. The Italians called him Arnoldo. His shop was always filled and the banter was constant. When the race results would come in over the radio, everything got quiet. Arnold's reaction was always the same. His foreign concoction of "godammit" would always come out "god dawgit." It could be good or bad. A ten length victory or a loss at the wire would be greeted with Arnold's "god dawgit." I also interpreted Arnold's slang as his desire to remain pure in the eyes of his Americani customers by not cursing an American "godammit" in public. At Christmas time Arnold would sell Christmas trees on the lawn in the front of his shop. According to his son Lou, invariably he gave away half the trees to friends and customers who needed a boost. He was always about giving.

Uncle Arnold would always come up to our house on

Hilton Street late in the evening after he closed up shop. There, he would hold court with a few cronies and visit with his parents. Arnold knew a little bit about everything. He had minimal formal education and none at all in America. He spoke broken English that meshed with a hacking smoker's cough, that produced his own dialect. He never had a harsh word for me or for anyone, for that matter. Arnold remained sharp by listening and dealing with the

Paul Cummings, Sr., Lolli's protagonist

Americani who came into his shop. Paul Cummings Sr., always quick with Gleason-like humor, tried to get Lolli's goat. But, always in a good way. He learned, literally "on his feet," listening and trimming hair. My father, who had a high school education and was well-read and up-to-date on things, never hesitated to banter with Arnold on any subject. He was street smart and easy-going. His passion was the race track. He loved the "cavali." On his rare days off, you knew where he was going. And, in later years, Lou would take him to the Maryland tracks. Italians love to gamble. It seems inherent in their nature. They took the first big gamble in coming over here, sight unseen. Remember that Columbus guy. It is no wonder that, on Ellis Island, the Italians would bet on the outcome of the guards' softball games, wagering cigarettes, coins and fruit. Arnold was of that genre, for sure.

As I grew older I became more observant. On evenings

when Arnold would come over for a cup of the black java, he would empty his pockets. Hundreds of little slips of paper would be spread out on the table. In winter, the seams of the furnace would emit an eerie glow as Arnold tabulated the day's catch. In summer, Adelina would divert the electric fan to keep the slips from blowing off the table. Like most Italian barbers, Arnold Lolli was a neighborhood bookmaker. Sort of a one-stop shopping trip. A trim and a bet. No wonder Lolli's Barber Shop on Saturday mornings looked like a beehive. Eventually he got caught. The Baltimore City Police Department Vice Squad, headed by the notorious blowhard, Captain Alexander Emerson, had been tracking him for some time. One night in the late 40's, I was awakened from a sound sleep by a loud thumping noise. Emerson and his goons were at our cellar door wielding his infamous maul hammer. Arnold, Aunt Anna and Adelina were in hysterical disarray. Anna was stuffing betting slips down her dress. Arnold was burning slips at the stove and Adelina was brandishing a huge iron

Captain Emerson

Captain Emerson was the "Elliott Ness" of his time, raiding and arresting everything that moved. He made a name for himself by pinching small time operators. His trademark was his surprise raid featuring an eight-pound maul hammer. He was condemned by the Baltimore City Bar Association for outrageous acts of vandalism in obtaining convictions.
Baltimore News American, circa 1958.

skillet and cursing in her best Abbrusezze. She looked like a crazed Viking in battle. None of the police touched her. I stood transfixed as they cuffed Uncle Arnold and whisked him and the remaining slips out the splintered cellar door. The ladies were cussing and crying as the sound of Emerson's squad car sirens fractured the still night. It was like a scene from an Italian opera.

I think Arnold did a few brief stints usually getting out early for good behavior. He was the house barber. When Grandpop Lolli passed away in 1951, he was laid out right at home as was the custom in those days. The open casket was right in the parlor. People would come to visit and pay their respects. The Italian relatives and close friends would eventually go down to the cellar for coffee, vino or both. It was a garish scene. A dead person, one you knew and loved, laying right there in the parlor. The house was inundated with flowers. In those days everybody smoked. Our house was devastated for weeks to come. But the scene of scenes was Uncle Arnold, coming from the penitentiary shackled in gray coveralls. Accompanied by several "Marshals," you would have thought he was Al Capone. I guess he was one of Emerson's prizes. I was around 16 and didn't know whether to laugh or cry. The Marshals loosened his shackles, the assemblage parted as Arnold went directly to his father's bier, said a prayer, hugged everybody, sipped a black cup, smoked a Lucky, and was back out the door and gone in a flash. By today's standards his treatment was barbaric. Where was Guy Sardella, Baltimore's Italian political Gadfly, when you needed him? Probably at the race track.

As time passed, Arnoldo went "straight" and moved his family farther into the suburbs. He opened a new shop in

Catonsville, hired a few assistants and began to retire. Arnold was always up on sports, particularly baseball, football and boxing. His opinions were always insightful. He spent his final years in the company of his wife Anna, and his sister and brother in-law, Mary and Paul Baker, plus his lifetime compare and race track crony, Bernard Manelli. A few years before he passed away, Arnold had been ill with colon and lung cancer. I went to St. Agnes Hospital to say good-bye. It was 1987. He was 78. Seemingly in a coma, the nun said he was cognizant and could hear you, but he didn't have much time left. He called me Son-ee, his dialectic spin on my nickname Sonny. He looked like there was no life left in him. But, when I grasped his hand, his grip was hard and strong. Uncle Arnold was not ready to leave. He lived two more years after coming home from St. Agnes. Anna took care of her husband of 54 years at home.

Starting in 1969, Arnoldo made eight trips back to Italy. But he always returned. I guess you could say he died an American. And a very good one. "Lolli," "Lolli The Barber," left a legacy of three loving children and seven grandchildren. He was special. A link between the old country and our world. Millions like him made America work. A mere blip on the screen, hardly. When he passed away, the Sons of Italy Lodge turned out in full force. The funeral cortege stretched for blocks to honor Arnoldo.

Uncle Marion

"He represents Little Italy for what it was and, in soul and spirit, still is – a place where Italians sunk their roots into this country."

On the corner of Fawn and Exeter Streets is an old store front. Across the faded Coca-Cola signboard is the name, Mugavero's. The door opens and a tiny bell jingles to announce your arrival. Inside a soft Sinatra ballad and the smell of hot coffee welcomes you to a time gone by. Standing behind the lunch counter wearing a clean white apron is Marion Mugavero, a full-blooded Sicilian, seventy-seven going on fifty. Known to all in Little Italy simply as Mugs, he bought the store in 1947 after mustering out of the Coast Guard following World War Two. Mugs is the unofficial king of Little Italy. A guy who typifies the indestructible nature of the neighborhood. Everybody knows him. From the neuvo-restaurant valet parkers to the life-long residents, everyone ventures into Mug's domain for soda, cigarettes or whatever. Everyone has their own spin on Mugs. Through the years he has helped many people in small but meaning-ful ways. Behind his caustic, old-world facade is a caring person if you are not turned off by his demeanor. In the sports vernacular he is a throwback. The poster of Rocky Marciano sets a tone for the store. From the wooden phone booth in the corner with its rounded bench seat, beaded tin

51

walls and accordion glass door to the terrazzo floor (especially poured by his neighborhood boys back in 1950) and pre-war glass cabinets, the place takes you back to another moment in time.

Mugs was born halfway down the block at 913 Fawn Street in 1925, the eighth of nine children. At the end of the block is the famous Sabatino's Ristorante, host to the nation's top celebs of their day, Sinatra, Agnew, Bennett, DiMaggio, et al. I remember when Sabatino's was Louge's Confectionery with swinging saloon doors, sawdust floors, pinball machines, soda coolers and a penny candy counter. Old man Louge wore a green visor and had a metal change dispenser secured to his belt. He never smiled. After the War he was gone, just about the time that Marion opened at the other end of the block. I can swear that some of the old wire-backed chairs in Mugs store are the exact ones that used to be in Louge's. Mugs just shrugs at the suggestion.

His lunch counter has eight permanent stools. Behind the counter is a tiny stove and a compact refrigerator. Sausage, meatball, and Italian cold-cut subs are dispensed daily. That's it. No menu, no side orders, no price list and no B.S. The bread is always fresh, the drinks cold, and the ingredients perfect. His customers request a sandwich, they don't order it. And only after the "opening dialogue" breaks the ice can one talk about ingredients, drinks, etc. And price is never mentioned. You give Mugs money and sometimes he gives you change.

He presides over his domain, fifty-five years and counting. Sometimes pompous, sometimes on the soapbox, always with his spin on the subject at hand. Always reducing the common denominator to the average Joe.

Mugs doesn't like big shots, bureaucrats, or celebrities. He can spot a phony the moment his front foot hits the terrazzo floor. He stands old-fashioned and proud, a throwback in stark contrast to the chic gold mine restaurants of Little Italy. He represents Little Italy for what it was, and in soul and spirit, still is – a place where Italians sunk their roots into this country.

Looking fit and much younger than his age, Mugs still has

Mugs... he stands old fashioned and proud, a throwback in stark contrast to the chic gold mine restaurants of Little Italy.

his hair, most of his teeth and all of his faculties. His wide shoulders and handsome Italian features keep him looking young. Double knee replacements haven't slowed him down one bit. After he returned from his surgeries, Josie and Helen, his loving sisters, placed a Sacred Heart of Jesus statue with flowers and a holy card in the corner of the store across from the phone booth. With that kind of support and the St. Leo's Church less than one hundred feet from his door, there is no telling how long Mugavero's Confectionery will last. In the meantime, fifties hits and Italian music are on the radio, the sauce is simmering, and time stands still.

The Cedrones

"His bride Lucia Mazzola had reservations about coming to America until Poppy laid down the law, 'Suffer in Italy without me, or prosper in America with me.' She got the message."

On a Sunday Morning in the 50's after Mass, Poppy would enter the bustling dining room filled with his children and their spouses. For a brief moment there was a respectful silence. Poppy would smile, then the banter, as if on cue, would resume. Poppy was Louis Cedrone, a stone mason by trade, from the southern mountain region of San Donato, 96 kilometers south east of Rome. Just before World War I (around 1914) he settled in Baltimore and eventually bought property way out in the country in what is today Hunt Valley. It was an area filled with limestone, marble and granite. Poppy and his crew of fellow immigrants laid cobblestone all over the city of Baltimore before and after the War, all the way up to the Great Depression. Whenever my wife and I see cobblestone streets in our travels, we always think of Poppy.

In the early years, the Cedrones lived in a tiny house on the rim of Little Italy around Lloyd and Granby Streets. A struggling family, they all chipped in to make things work. In 1930 Poppy moved his family out of Little Italy. He bought some ground out in Govans and proceeded to build a stone house with his bare hands at 5653 Govane Avenue. He and Lucia started to raise a family of nine children, several of whom were born in Italy. Poppy traveled back and forth to Italy in the early years after the War, bringing home money earned in America. His bride, Lucia Mazzola, had reservations about coming to America until Poppy laid down the law, "Suffer in Italy without me, or prosper in America with me." She got the message. Lucia was a lot like my grandmother Adelina who always felt trapped in America. Lucia ran her growing household with old world discipline and austerity. This was a woman who sewed spoons, knives and forks from the boat into the hem of her skirt, proclaiming, "We will need them more than they will and besides, they won't miss them." At home she cracked the whip but Poppy always had the last word and his humanity softened Lucia's hard edge. He even allowed the girls to attend public school to escape the wrath

La Famiglia Cedrone. From left to right... Connie, Danny, Clara, Angeline, Josephine, Poppy and his wife Lucy Mazzola Cedrone. The Cedrones would eventually have four more children. (Note Poppy's "Stone Mason" hands.)

and corporal punishment of the St. Leo's School nuns.

Poppy was a short, powerful little guy with a sunny disposition. As a young man he had dark curly hair and a handlebar mustache that typified the Southern Italian Immigrant. He loved opera and all types of

Poppy playing his "Squeeze box" for youngest daughter Lucille and, in the background, grand daughter Kathy.

music. For years he played his accordion and sang at parties and family gatherings. In his later years, as his hair turned snowy white, he walked all over Govans and points north and south. A trait his son Lou exhibits to this day.

At night Poppy would sip the "Grappa" and play his squeeze box, watching his children grow up American. World War II was on the horizon. Seeking the American Dream, the Cedrone children were conservative, hard workers who gravitated to the arts. They were engrossed in music, movies, and live entertainment. The third oldest daughter, Clara, became a professional night club entertainer and singer, traveling on the cruise ship circuit. She also flew all over the world working for the USO. She lived in Greenwich Village. Lou Cedrone, Jr., for many years, was the noted and highly respected film critic for the Baltimore Sun. He and his American wife, Nancy Nelson Cedrone, are world travelers. Henry Cedrone was an accomplished musician and band leader who sang and played several instruments. In his younger days he worked the County and Western circuit as a backup for Tex Ritter. Danny, the oldest son seemed most like Poppy in looks, demeanor and work ethic. For over 40-years he worked in the bowels of the Bethlehem Steel works. He still found time to perform in amateur productions. Multi-talented, he could act, sing, produce and direct. And, like his younger brother Lou, served in World War II.

Josephine, the oldest daughter married Harry Presti, a successful furniture salesman whose family were Sicilians from Cefalu. They traveled around the world and wintered in Florida, living a great life. Jo was very proud of her family and very giving. Poppy's second oldest daughter, Angeline, was called "Ann" or "Nanny." An avid card player, she raised two children and always cooked up a storm. Her daughter, Wesley, who was a student in my History class at Towson Catholic High School, introduced me to her cousin, Connie, whom I quickly married. Nanny, who was a widow, took in several of my Baltimore University basketball players as boarders over the years. The most notable being Steve Varanko, who stayed in town and is now our accountant. Philomena, for many years, worked at Social Security. She and her

Lou Cedrone, Jr., the son of an Italian immigrant, proudly served in the U.S. Army during World II. Above, he is pictured, ironically, as part of the Allied occupation force in Rome, less than 100 kilometers from his ancestral roots.

58

husband, Al Forgione, who was from New York, raised four very successful children. Lucille, the baby of the family, is the Official Archivist, who, to this day, keeps the family on the same page throughout the years.

In 1964, I married Constance Peddicord, whose mother Connie was Poppy's fourth daughter. She raised five successful children and has eleven grandchildren of her own. She makes a big thing out of my being Italian and it always makes me feel good.

Poppy was more than just a laborer. He admired and studied the great architecture of the times. The Radio City Music Hall, along with the George Washington and Verrazano Bridges fascinated him. In another time and place he could have been a very successful architect. Two of his great grandsons must carry some of his genes. Thomas Peddicord III graduated Summa Cum Laude from the University of Virginia and is employed by the Ford Motor Company in Dearborn, Michigan as an Automotive Architect. Younger brother Joseph Peddicord follows his brother to Virginia and has designs on a career in music.

Poppy passed away in 1971. His growing legacy numbers nine children, seventeen grandchildren, and twenty-eight great, great grandchildren..

Several years ago, after his passing, the children got together and sold the rocky parcel of ground out in Hunt Valley where Poppy once mined stone to ply his trade. They divided the proceeds into equal shares.

Another part of his legacy is the Annual Cedrone Christmas party that is still going strong. The tradition extended into the 21st Century with the latest event. A long way from the original boat ride.

On the occasion of the 50th Wedding Anniversary of "Poppy & Lucia", the Cedrones gathered for a Golden Celebration at the Park Plaza Hotel. (Back row, from left) Clara Cedrone Mitchell, Harry Presti, Josephine Cedrone Presti, Tom Peddicord, Connie Cedrone Peddicord, Henry Cedrone, Danny Cedrone, Ann Cedrone Dodson, Al Forgione, Philomena Cedrone Forgione. (Front row) Lucille Cedrone, Bud Dodson, June Butler Cedrone, Louis Cedrone (Poppy), Lucia Mazzola Cedrone, Louise Marziali Cedrone, Lou Cedrone, Jr.

Section II

"Così Italiano"

Things Italian

Sabatino

"There was no television then so my entertainment was to sit at the top of the cellar steps and listen to the Italians."

Sabatino Luperini came over from Italy with some family money. He was not a pick and shovel, pre-World War I immigrant. Well-dressed and personable, yet he was not afraid to get his hands dirty. To make a living he owned a few hole-in-the-wall dives. One was the Lighthouse Hotel on East Pratt Street where Harbor Place now stands. It was a redneck Country and Western bar with live music. The other was the The Moonglow Café on Pennsylvania Avenue in the heart of Baltimore's Negro Gold Coast. An Italian immigrant doing business with hillbillies and Blacks. He had a raspy rat-a-tat voice that could speak several Italian dialects, broken English and a semblance of American conversational, all with flair. He was a flashy sort of dresser, old world Italian with a continental pizzazz. He clearly had a foot on each continent. Sabatino was stocky but not small, thick but not heavy, with noble Roman features. He was born in a tiny mountain village called Vicopisano near Pisa.

After work Sabatino always made a late stop at our house. There in our basement he would have a homemade wine or espresso. Stuff he couldn't get in his own places. When Sabatino settled in, he would climb the "soap box" and

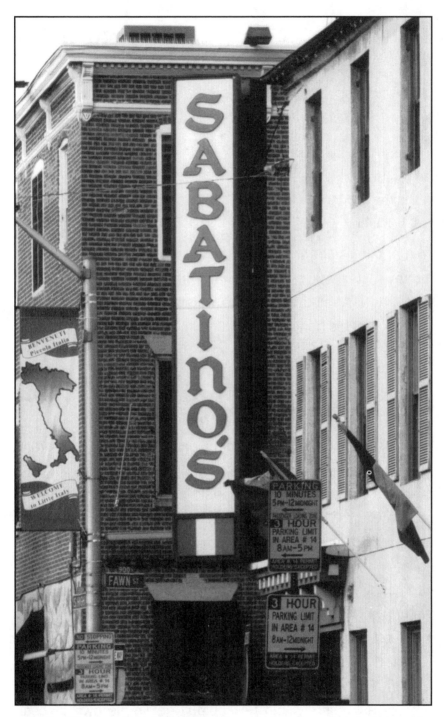

Today, the Little Italy restaurant that bears Sabatino's Luperini's name is a Baltimore institution, with thousands making their way to its Fawn Street location.

launch into his latest tirade. Usually it was politics. Sabatino would always bring me liquor corks by the bag full. Back in the 40's there were no hi-tech plastics. The corks had a colorful wooden brand logo on the caps. I would use them as toy soldiers or barricades around my play forts. He knew that I always waited up for them. But more than the corks I liked to listen to his soap box oratory. Over the drone of the oil burner Sabatino would give his state of the union address. Adelina would pour the drinks and put out Italian cookies. She called him "Sabetta." Grandpop Lolli, Arnoldo, Bernard, and whoever else had stopped in would listen in rapt attention then try to get a word in edgewise usually to no avail. In winter the visits were short. In summer they went into the night. There was no television then so my entertainment was to sit at the top of the cellar steps and listen to the Italians.

One day Sabatino brought his oldest son, Joseph, over for a visit. What a shock that was. Joseph was a completely Americanized teenager in an ivy league suit, with soft features, impeccable manners and no rat-a-tat delivery. Evidently Sabatino and his Sicilian wife, Francesca, both first generation Italians, wasted no time in raising their children American. They lived on South Hilton Street and were members of the St. Johns parish in the Lexington Market area where it was said that more Sicilians from Cefalu lived than in Cefalu itself. Sabby followed Francesca home from the movies one day and the rest is history. He and Uncle Arnold were buddies. They and their wives would go to the Edgewood on Edmondson Avenue to see American movies. But Sabatino loved the old Italian country songs of Carlo Buti whom I have affectionately named the Italian Hank Williams.

Back in the 50's Sabby met a fellow paison named Joe

Canzani, the chef at Velleggia's, and they became partners in an Italian restaurant – using Joe's cooking skills and Sabatino's cash and business acumen. Finding a spot on the corner of Fawn and High Streets, the former site of Louge's Confectionery, they opened Sabatino's in 1954. It quickly became the "in place" to eat and be seen. Former Maryland Governor and U.S. Vice-President

Sabatino Luperini

Spiro Agnew was a fixture at Sabatino's in those days. He and Sabby were close and had many long political "debates" at the restaurant. It is even said that Agnew, upon his resignation of the Vice-Presidency on October 10, 1973, returned immediately to Sabatino's where he found comfort. Also friendly with Sabatino was Odell Smith, a noted political speech writer who served under Governor Mandel and other major politicos. Sabatino spent his later years visiting his native Vicopisano every spring. He could never quite get Italia out of his veins. At the height of its popularity other prominent people such as Mayor Schaefer, and celebs like Sinatra, Di Maggio, and Tony Bennett ate at Sabatino's. But Sabby never gave any of them a bag of cork bottle stoppers.

Now nearly a half century later it is still the "in place." Sabatino sold his interest in the early 70's. He learned the American game and how to play it. But, when I drive through Little Italy now and see the flashing neon sign, my thoughts go back over 50 odd years to the Lolli's basement, the Carlo Buti records and Mr. Sabatino Luperini.

La Donna Frumane

"La Donna was Mother Theresa before Mother Theresa was invented."

Still too young for school, I hung around the house with Adelina. She would go for morning coffee with Mrs. Bossi four doors down while I rode my tricycle up and down the sidewalks of Hilton Street. In those days salesmen were always on the loose. When they saw Mrs. Lolli they backed off. Still, we had our regulars. Tall, statesman-like, Mr. Shipley represented Metropolitan Life. He dressed like a rich banker and looked a little like F.D.R. We were part of his debit book. He was always very respectful of Mrs. Lolli, and she liked him too. I could tell because she actually went into her "broken English gig" for him. Maranto's always delivered the bread on Tuesdays and Thursdays. I got into the habit of breaking off the heel and pouring olive oil over the fresh bread, like the Italian chain restaurants do now a half century later. Whenever I did this I caught holy hell. It was bread for the table not to be picked at. The Hoffberger oil truck would pull up to the side of the house and fill our oil burner tank. I guess that's how they got the money to buy the Orioles.

Overall, Adelina was pretty good with salesmen. She always had a few choice mutterings after they left. But the one bugaboo that always appeared, usually at the wrong times, was the visit of La Donna Frumane. She was a member of some Italian order of nuns who would solicit funds from Italian-American families. She would make her way through the entire city. Wednesday must have been her West Baltimore day. La Donna Frumane was a tiny nun dressed from head to toe in black, replete with rosary beads and those ubiquitous black brogans. Her cassock hung down to ground level and when she walked she seemed battery-operated. La Donna had those sad, doleful eyes, a large nose and a sallow complexion and her voice had a sorrowful, moaning quality. She spoke no English. She was the perfect beggar. La Donna was Mother Teresa before Mother Teresa was invented. She was from Abruzzi like Adelina.

She had her ritual. First, she stood at the door without knocking as if we knew she was there. If the door didn't open she would tap once. As Grandma Lolli filled the threshold, many pleasantries were exchanged. She was invited in. Always she refused. Then, in an instant she would come in. I knew the drill. Finally, they would end up in the cellar drinking the black coffee. La Donna always liked a shot of anisette in the cold

Two ladies from Abruzzi...

Mrs. Manelli (left) and Adelina, two ladies from La Donna Frumane's native Abruzzi, share a smile and a warm day on the beach at Wildwood, NJ... Paulie Mugavero collection

months. She never produced any documents, booklets, or holy cards. When it was time to leave Adelina would reach under the top of her black dress and produce a few folded dollar bills. Then we got sort of a papal blessing in that Italian moan of hers and suddenly she was gone. She always stayed too long and tested Adelina's patience. I'm sure Grandmom would rather have answered the door bell and handed her the stash.

The Dancer

According to Anna Lolli, until Adelina broke her leg carrying me through the doorway at Hilton Street, despite her hefty frame, she was quite agile. She danced the Tarantella with a style that only natives from Abruzzi could. Placing hands on hips she would skip from side to side keeping her weight back on her heels all the while spinning in a tight circle. Transported back in time, she was especially animated when her son, Arnold, joined in the dance.

Some days when we saw La Donna motoring about the neighborhood Grandma would close the venetian blinds (only Italians had venetian blinds, it seemed), turn out the lights and sit quietly in the basement kitchen. We never knew from which door she would attempt her "assault." Some days she actually came in the back yard and knocked on the cellar door. Serving as the "point-man," I would sneak up to the parlor and peek out from the edge of the blinds. Sure enough there she was, a little nun doll standing motionless on the porch. One knock, then two knocks. I began to smile, then laugh. Grandma would appear at the top of the cellar steps motioning for me to be quiet and get away from the window. "Signora," "Signora Lolli," in that plaintive moan. By now I was giggling and so was Grandmom. Finally, she left. We did a little "Italian Tarantella" victory dance. But we kept the blinds shut for the rest of the day.

Bernardo

"He sort of marched along slowly, heavy in the heel and wary. Maybe it was from the countless hours on his feet in that sweat shop, or the subliminal knowledge that he was treading on foreign soil."

As I was growing up, there were dozens of people who came down to my grandparents' basement kitchen. The one guy I'll never forget was Bernard Manelli, a tiny, barrel-chested, old fashioned Italian. He was born in Philadelphia around 1912. The Manelli's were from Teramo, the same home town of the Lolli family.

Immigration patterns were familial, local, and regional. Most of my grandparents' original friends were people from the same town. They came over together, usually worked the same trade, and socialized together. They were, essentially, family. Bernard Manelli was family.

He worked for decades in a tailor shop as a presser foreman. Shortly after he divorced his wife, Tillie D'Alesio, he moved out to West Baltimore to live with his brother Alfred (Fi-Fi) and took his evening meal with the Lollis. I gravitated to Bernard easily. He was always telling me stories about his days in Italy as a cyclist and adventurer. He was so animated with my grandparents that his enthusiasm captivated me. Consequently, I hung on his every "broken English" word. Assimilation was not in his make-up. Bernard chain-smoked strong cigarettes and drank lots of black coffee. Still alive today at 90, he still speaks old country. He and Arnold were inseparable friends. Two old-fashioned Italians in an emerging America. Out of place and proud of it.

Bernard even had an old-world gait. He was never jaunty or on his toes. He sort of marched along slowly, heavy in the heel and wary. Literally a step away from poor soul status. Maybe it was from the countless hours on his feet in that sweat shop, or the subliminal knowledge that he was

Bernardo on the Board Walk in Atlantic City... surely on his way to "the track."

treading on foreign soil.

One summer day when I was around thirteen years old, I was coming home from Patterson Park on the # 20 bus. The #20 started out in East Baltimore, around Haven Street, and cut a swath directly through the heart of the city, from East to West, ten hard miles. Stopping every block, she picked up a diverse clientele. It was the working class of post war Baltimore.

Shoppers from Lexington and Hollins Markets mixed with department store shoppers and working stiffs to make the #20 Baltimore's busiest route. I was tucked into a tiny space in the back of the bus. It was oppressively hot. Busses were not air conditioned back then. The bus was filled with people and their packages. Somewhere around Eutaw Street, Bernard boarded the bus and seated himself on the side bench behind the driver. My immediate reaction was to call

out to him. But the bus was jam-packed and street noise permeated the air. It was impossible for me to join him up front with all the people standing in the aisles with packages and bags. So, for the next 20 minutes, I fixed my gaze on Bernard. He had long, slicked-back hair that was still damp from his day's work. His sharp, aquiline nose and neatly trimmed mustache set off his proud persona. His dark eyes stared straight ahead. He wore a white, short-sleeved silk shirt,

As young boys, Bernardo's son Rudy (right) and I became friends. Today, Rudy is a successful attorney in the Towson area... Paulie Mugavero collection

73

open at the neck, which accentuated his thick, hairy chest. Around his neck was a small neat red bandanna and a gold chain. The rest of the passengers paled in comparison to this "ethnic colossus" sitting at attention in the front of the bus. For 20 minutes, in wilting heat, amidst the noises and jostling, he never moved a muscle. Despite living in America, presumably with a better lifestyle, it became apparent to me on that bus ride that here was an Italian man – an Italian man forever trapped in a world not of his making. One who gives and takes, but never can take away the Italian in him. I also realized that this was the only time I saw Bernard without a cigarette.

Bernard had two brothers. Alfred, a tailor who chased the American Dream, married an American girl and raised a family. Gino is a nationally renowned landscape painter and, in his day, was an international bike racer who transcended any ethnic roots. Bernard was most happy with that Racing Form in his back pocket, sipping a black coffee and smoking a "Lucky," waiting for Arnold to pick him up to go to Pimlico. The race track was his only concession to America. My last word on Bernardo, "Recognize a child and you make a friend for life."

Vino

"...whenever I would grab a few grapes out of the crate, I was admonished. These Italians sure were serious about their wine."

Every Spring, Grandpop Lolli would make wine. The white grapes made clear, light wine, whereas the dark grapes made the Italian staple called "dago red." The process would start when a large produce truck pulled up to the garage and began to unload dozens of crates of light and dark grapes into our tiny back yard. Mr. Patsy (Pasquale), one of Grandpop's "gumbahs," would show up with the wine press. He was wiry, strong, with a thick, dark mustache. He wore a leather cap and a red bandanna was loosely wrapped around his neck. Patsy had done manual labor. He had no belly and just a few teeth. He was a presser in Grandpop's tailor shop. He had a great disposition, but whenever I would grab a few grapes out of the crate, I was admonished. These Italians sure were serious about their wine. The bulky wine press was dragged down the steps into the back cellar, where Mr. Patsy prepared the contraption. I think they wanted to squeeze their grapes in private instead of exposing their efforts to the Americani walking around out there. As long as I didn't snitch any grapes and stayed out of the way, I could watch until bedtime.

Mr. Patsy and the guys worked in their undershirts as they

alternated turning the iron wheel of the press, placing a wooden plank through the spokes to gain more leverage. It was Grandpop's project. His grapes and his house. Mr. Patsy seemed like a limited partner and all the others knew they could come over during the year to drink the "grappa." As Mr. Patsy gripped the wheel, other guys would break open the crates and spill grapes into the wheelhouse of the wine press. For the next few hours not a word of English was spoken as these boys "from the other side" went about their chore. Kibitzing and joking. The juice flowed from the bottom of the press through a strainer. Patsy used that bandana to wipe away the perspiration as another paison would take over the wheel. After a while, the smell of sweat and fermenting grapes would drive me upstairs. The Italians would work into the night. They would then sit around the cellar kitchen table, drinking that black brew, smoking cigars, and talking happy talk.

By the end of the week, the juice was in Grandpop Lolli's barrels and the yard was filled with broken crates and big cakes of rotting grape skins. I'm sure the Americani in the neighborhood thought those "dagos" were crazy. For the rest of the year, the wine flowed at the Lolli table. It was terrible tasting stuff. I noted that the only people who craved the "grappa" were native Italians, "born on the other side." My parents hated the stuff. But, for Lolli, Patsy and the "fratellos," it was an elixir. And a yearly ritual.

Joe D.

Throughout the neighborhood there were scattered Italian families. But there were no organized events or activities that bonded us together, like in Little Italy. Grandpop Lolli would play bocci and drink wine with his cronies and Adelina would attend novenas and visit with her contemporaries. These people were not assimilating themselves into American life. They were Italians living in another country. My parents were truly a generation in transition as they moved about freely in the mainstream of America, yet tied closely to their parental upbringing. In the meantime, I was quickly becoming Americanized. My school, St. Joseph's Monastery, had no ethnic strain to it. And, with my name being Baker, I was ostensibly vanilla. I was shocked to to find out my eighth-grade teacher thought I was Puerto Rican. But I was trapped in this "Italian thing," as my parents worked and I was raised by this Italian lady

Joe "The Italian Stallion" posing with Poppa DeFlavis.

77

who couldn't speak the language.

The War was winding down. There was no TV or Sports Illustrated and all the household names in the sports world were in the service. In this atmosphere, a pre-teenager had to find his own role model. Up the street lived an Italian family named DeFlavis. Their children were older than I. Mr. and Mrs. DeFlavis were friends of my grandparents. They wore the same uniform and spoke the same language. One of my distressing moments would always be when Grandma Adelina would meet up with a fellow countryman in a store, at a bus stop, or on the street, and they would begin their dialectic banter. I was too young to leave her side, and it seemed like every Americani in the neighborhood would be walking by, staring at this "old world" reunion. Joe De Flavis was a teenager no longer joined at the hip with his parents. He was free to roam the streets as an American. I envied him. Joe was a stocky, barrel-chested little guy with an energized motor. He was always working a job somewhere. Usually in construction. He never went to high school that I knew of. I was too young to get his attention other than a passing nod as he motored down the street to catch the bus.

Tape Ball

It was not uncommon in the 40's to play with a baseball whose cover was "knocked-off" and replaced with tar tape wound around it.

Joe would always have a cigarette behind his ear. One summer afternoon, the neighborhood teenagers gathered on the skin diamond behind P.S. #91 school for a game of hardball. Word spread throughout the neighborhood. Glen Granger had come home from work with two new baseballs he bought at French's Sporting Goods on Baltimore Street near Eutaw. All the participants would pitch in to defray the cost, and for the privilege of playing with a new baseball. In those days a neighborhood game was a big thing. I was so excited that I broke my parents rule to "never cross Hilton Street alone." But, to get to the #91 field I had to do it. At age nine it was like Caesar crossing the Rubicon.

As the players were warming up, a cheer went out as a bare-chested, paint-smeared image came jogging into focus. It was Joe De Flavis, fresh off the construction site, ready for action. An immediate argument broke out over which team would get Joe. It wasn't a case of an Italian being accepted, but a full-fledged argument over who would get him. Didn't these guys know Joe's mom and dad couldn't speak English and wore those dark clothes? Somehow in this setting it just didn't matter. In Little Italy all the kids were Italian. Strength in numbers, customs and friendships. But outside Little Italy it was not as easy to be Italian. But Joe, the Italian Stallion, was an equal. I learned something that day.

What he did that day was catch behind the plate without a mask, a cigarette dangling from his lips, scooping a pitch out of the dirt barehanded, then smashing a fast ball over the fence. He then was the first to climb over and find the new baseball. In 1945, role models and heroes were hard to find. Joe filled the bill big time and all the Americani loved him.

A few years later on a Sunday at Bloomingdale Oval hundreds of fans gathered around the gridiron, five deep, to watch Arcadia play Wildwood in a sandlot football game. In those days it was called semi-pro. These games were the precursors of what was to come after the War. Every play was met with raucous cheering from the sidelines. Several times the referees would have to stop play and move the fans back behind the restraining ropes. Teenage girls and young women would be wearing corsages with ribbons in the colors of their favorite team. Large crowds gathered. There were no face masks and all the players wore black eye shadow. The action was fast and furious. You could see, hear and practically feel the hits as the players moved with an aggressive purpose. Late in the game Arcadia moved ahead. The sun was going down and the long shadows brought a chill into the air. Back on the goal line was a stocky, little halfback with powerful legs. There was something familiar about him, but in that theatrical football costume, my senses were clouded. He fielded the kick-off cleanly and bolted forward like a cannon shot, swerving left at the twenty toward the far sideline. Getting to the corner before the puffing Arcadians, he turned on a burst of speed that rendered the other 21 players motionless. Ninety-five yards untouched. As he jogged back to the sidelines I noticed that familiar "catch the bus trot." Running down the sidelines to better observe the celebration, the hero riding the shoulders of his teammates removed his helmet. Incredulously, I saw that it was none other than Joe DiFlavis, truly the Italian Stallion. Just a few blocks away, Momma DiFlavis was fixing an Italian supper and Pop was on his porch smoking a DiNobili totally oblivious to Joe "out playin' ball." This scenario made me realize the cultural differences. Children of Italian descent could assimilate and become Americans rather easily with each passing generation despite their parents. I never saw Joe DeFlavis much after I grew up and never really met him. I knew his parents better from the "corner meetings" and visits to our house. Joe was my first hero and he was real. I saw him perform up close and personal. Joe became a fire fighter.

A Pedestal in the Garden of Eden

"If it could talk, it would tell the story of our family."

Louis and Adelina Lolli came to America just before World War I, around 1912. They were from Teramo and Pescara in the province of Abruzzi, on the Adriatic coast of Italy. Just a few miles apart and halfway up the boot, they were city dwellers who lived a comfortable life. As a rule, the farther south you go in Italy the higher the level of poverty. The Sicilians, for the most part, were dirt-poor and were being pushed off their lands by a criminal element. The Lolli's had it pretty good.

Grandpop Lolli was a master tailor. When he arrived stateside in Philadelphia, he followed friends to the Baltimore area. He found a plot of ground in the "campagna" (Country), near Westminster, Maryland in a place called Union Bridge. There he started a small garment factory employing a dozen or so immigrants. They lived on a small farm in southwest Baltimore. When the factory burned down they sold the farm and moved to 18 North Hilton Street in West Baltimore. The master tailor went to work as a sweat shop foreman. The Hilton Street location was a corner row house with a front and side yard. Adelina Lolli planted so many flowers and bushes in the small front yard you could hardly walk through the rose bushes, hydrangea plants and wandering fauna. On the side yard was the exalted fig tree, surrounded by peppermint plants, and wrapped in cloth armhole bastings during the winter.

Because of all the plants, it was most difficult to cut the remaining grass. A hedge bordered the front yard. Early on, I called it the Garden of Eden after the well-known Bible story. Directly in the center of the Garden of Eden was a concrete pedestal reinforced with iron rods and decorated with pieces of cut glass and blue plaster. Ever since I can remember, this old world relic held forth in the middle of the Garden of Eden. At various times it served as a pedestal for a statue of the Virgin Mary, a bird bath, and most of the time it was a plant holder. It was in our yard as early as The Great Depression in 1932 - a unique Italian sentinel exposed to all the elements. I remember mowing the lawn around it. Moving it was an impossible task. The base of the pedestal contained a slab of concrete and was reinforced by some brutal iron. If it could talk, it would tell the story of our family.

In 1956 we moved to the suburbs. Grandpop Lolli had passed away in 1951. Adelina wasn't feeling well, my Dad was still working 60 hours a week, and my mom was working full-time in the tailor shop. I now had a driver's license and a car, and my little sister was being bussed to a fancy Catholic school. In the dynamics of "Italians moving," it must have been Ellis Island revisited. Everything was bundled and hauled away. Somehow the pedestal probably camouflaged in the Garden of Eden didn't make it. It was not missed early on and was soon forgotten.

We got on with our lives. Grandma passed away in 1964, the year I got married. We had three kids and moved to West

Virginia for eight years, and my sister was in California. Through the years, I would come across the pedestal in family photos and wonder what ever became of that Italian relic. My parents moved to a retirement community in the 1980's.

In the mid-90's, driving through West Baltimore, I drove through the old neighborhood. Driving down Hilton Street, I turned right onto Elbert Street to view our old corner house. The front yard was devastated, the hedge was reduced to dead twigs and grass was nonexistent. Many houses were boarded up and the old neighborhood had seen better days. The overview was sad. But when I zeroed in on the old property, there it was as big as life. The pedestal from the Garden of Eden was standing erect like a beacon in the wilderness. It had been sitting there for 40 years (1956-1996). Part of it's bowl was broken off and several steel rods were exposed on her flanks where the concrete and cut glass had lost its battle with the elements.

The neighborhood had entirely changed and I was a little nervous. The house was peppered with spray paint and I wasn't about to rap on the front door. I drove over to Monastery Avenue to seek the advice of Mike Clark, a highly educated and erudite hermit/bachelor still living in the house where he was born and raised. We had been childhood friends. I explained my dilemma. Mike sized up the situation in an instant. Off we went. Pulling into Elbert Street, Mike ordered me to "open the trunk." As he marched through the dead hedgerow toward the pedestal the owner pulled up in his car. Without breaking stride Mike spoke out telling the owner that "he" pointing to me, "used to live here and came back to pick up this old piece of concrete." Gaining his incredulous assent, Mike, who was a power lifter before weights were in vogue, now age 60, straddled the pedestal, clean and jerked it to chest level, and quickly strode to the car where he dropped it into the trunk   The shocks of my Buick Riviera were tested to the max as Mike said, "Let's get the #!?*#*! out of here."

It was meant to be. A link with the past. I had the bowl repaired, left the rods exposed and the glass un-replaced. Now, on spring mornings in my back yard I have a piece of Adelina's Garden of Eden.   Connie has also successfully planted hydrangea bushes nearby.

P.S. Upon reaching it's final destination, two of my strong, body-building sons could not budge the pedestal. We had to get a wheelbarrow. Thank you Mike.

That's me (left), circa 1944, viewing the pedestal. And, in 1998 (right), I posed with my grandson Jacob and the "recovered" pedestal... 54 years later... Paulie Mugavero collection

Adelina's Nephew

"His voice resonated through the halls of Villa Pace. He clearly had a future."

Italians in America kept close ties to the Old Country. In between World Wars, some would actually travel back and forth across the ocean every few years. Relatives would come for visits, and men would come over to work, then send money back to their families in Italy. An exercise Christopher Columbus would have approved. And there were many circumstances where certain members of a family refused to budge on the issue of immigration and families were split up. As a result there were Italian men who ended up with two families on two continents.

Adelina and Luigi had left their two young sons, Arnoldo and Nicola, back in Teramo, while they sought to establish roots in America. Could they afford America? Would they like it? In 1928, Adelina went back to bring the boys to America. Arnoldo, then eighteen, was very upset. He had begun to establish a life in Italy. The younger Nicola easily complied. Adelina's family was happy-go-lucky and not the poorest of the poor. They hated to see them all go off to America. Throughout the year, particularly after they developed a solid base, Adelina would always "send something home." In between the pages of a long letter would be a five or a ten spot. A lot of money in those days. Years later, when Anna, Arnold's wife, went over to Teramo, she would meet the relatives who were "sick" and in need of money for "prescriptions." "They looked pretty damn healthy to me," noted Anna. Adelina always remembered her roots and never seemed to mind being hoodwinked. She would say, "Maybe the prescriptions worked."

Her biggest undertaking came in 1960 when she sent for her brother's son, one Gaspari Cantoressi, a tiny thirty-two-year-old dynamo with a booming tenor voice. Gaspari, who quickly became "Casper" to his American relatives, had formal operatic training. He was special. It was never really clear as to whether Casper wanted to come over in the first place. But Adelina, seeing an opportunity to help her family cash in on Casper's talent, initiated the undertaking. No

Adelina (left) beams with pride in the presence of her nephew Gaspari Cantoressi. Blessed with a magnificent tenor voice, "Casper" came to America at the request of Adelina to pursue fame and fortune as an Opera star (On right as Rudolph in La Boheme). His heart, however, remained in Italy with his young wife and, after just four months, he left America and the stage for good.

sooner than he arrived, Arnold, Anna and Adelina, with the help of Italian bigwigs Guy Sardella and Frank Della Noce, set up a meeting at Villa Pace with the retired world famous soprano, Rosa Ponselle. Ponselle was captivated by the little curly-haired tenor. His voice resonated through the halls of Villa Pace. He clearly had a future. A few weeks later, Ponselle set up a second visit and produced a soprano to sing duets with Casper. Things were cooking.

Arnold bought Casper a piano and Adelina put him up in his own guest quarters at the home of a friend. At the time, I was in my early twenties, seeking my own "American Dream" and struggling through. I was not about to pal around with some tiny foreign opera singer who wore funny clothes and couldn't speak English. I was mannerly but distant from this process. I surely owed my grandmother more, but she placed no demands on me. Looking back, I regret my unwillingness to help Casper find himself. I just didn't have the confidence then.

As weeks wore on, Casper became distant. Unable to speak the language and with no outlets beyond family, he began to yearn for home. He had a genuine talent and passion for music. But no one ever ascertained whether he aspired to the stage. And no one realized the tremendous pull coming from Italia. Casper had married his high school sweetheart, Ida, prior to coming over. After four months, he was back home for good, leaving everyone baffled, particularly Ponselle who kept calling the Lolli's for the whereabouts of that "powerful little tenor."

Adelina put out a lot of time and energy, to say nothing of the money, money she didn't have to spare, to bring her nephew over. Everyone was drained by the process. An

87

opera within an opera. Everyone on this side of the water was mad, except for Arnold, who was never judgmental. After all, he himself was forced to come over here as a young man against his wishes. So Arnold kept the relationship going with his cousin, sending "stuffed envelopes" and traveling to Italy many times for visits. Ten years after his return to Italy, Casper said to Arnold one summer night in Teramo over vino, "Un calcio nel culo e lascia dentro il piede." "Kick me in the ass hard and leave the shoe in it.

Casper became a music teacher. He and Ida raised two daughters and are proud grandparents. He never came back to America. He and Anna still stay in touch.

Mangia

"Sometimes she would make tiny meatballs by the dozens, no larger than a marble, and sprinkle them over the macaroni and sauce."

The Italian celebrations at holidays and many Sundays featured an abundance of food, very little of which I liked. I was too close to the process. Too much sauce, too much cheese, and the ever present chicken.

Early on, I liked all the American stuff my upwardly mobile parents fed me on trips and outings. When it came to the Italian "abundanza" I was unimpressed.

To my recollection neither of my Italian grandmothers were great cooks but I was too young to accurately judge. Adelina was always cooking. I would wake up on weekends and some week days to the aroma of peppers and eggs sizzling away in garlic and olive oil. The food was always old fashioned and plentiful. One time she fixed bracciolle (a thin steak rolled up with varied ingredients inside), and wrapped it up with Grandpop's buttonhole thread to hold it together while it cooked. Bracciolle is usually wrapped with a thick string. . . even I knew that. Hardly visible, many of us practically choked on the silk thread. The best Italian treat was the bread from Maranto's delivered in mid-afternoon. Two Italian and one Sicilian. The loaves were crusty and warm and Adelina would pour olive oil and sprinkle grated cheese over the slices and we would have a great pre-dinner treat. The only time I remember that she ever laid hands on me was one afternoon when I ate over half a loaf right on the front porch. She was expecting company and would be short of bread. I also learned a few new words that day. The Sicilian bread was very coarse and tight in texture. The olive oil could hardly penetrate and it was hard to chew, as most things Sicilian are.

The desserts were also disappointing. Not sweet enough for Lord Fauntleroy. The cannoli had too much ricotta cheese, the cookies were too dry and doughy without enough icing, and the fruit and nut bars could break your teeth. All this stuff they dipped in thick, dark coffee. The only things I liked were Chef Boy-Ar-Dee in a can (a sweet tomato taste and no cheese), and Royal Crown Cola (ice cold to Americanize my taste buds). All of this could have been my way of showing independence. Whenever brought to task I would say, "This Chef Boy-Ar-Dee guy was Italian wasn't he?"

My mother worked in a sweat shop her entire life and when she married my father, she was lucky she could boil an egg. But, as time wore on and Adelina grew older Mom began to cook and bake and by the time I left the house at 28, she had developed into an outstanding cook. Likewise, my wife never learned to cook from her mother, who was also Italian

Ettori Boiardi

Ettori Boiardi, an immigrant chef, opened a restaurant in Cleveland and by 1930 started putting pasta and sauce in cans. During World War II, Chef Boyardee was the largest supplier of rations for the U.S. and Allied forces.

First and second generation Italians, under pain of death, would never buy a can. Thank God for the Americani.

but who cooked right from the book for an American husband. But, as she raised our three sons, she began to cook in earnest and in fact, learned how to make many of my mother's Italian specialties. However, to her chagrin I still prefer plain spaghetti, meatballs and fresh bread.

Pizza didn't come to the American market place til after World War II. It could be found in "Little Italy's" all over the country, but not in the universal manner which we now know.

My first pizza encounter came in South Philadelphia in 1946, while visiting cousin Mimmi Lolli. His son, Richard, took me to a neighborhood row house where the warm aroma of fresh dough wafted up from the cellar. A kid in a white apron was hoisting the pies up to the street from the oven below. The smell was better than the pizza. Lots of tomato, cheese, and enough oregano to choke a horse. Boiling hot, the first bite burned the roof of my mouth badly. As a kid, I was a bad Italian. Now, in the twilight, I begin to appreciate so much more, things Italian.

Adelina and Luigi, would make Italian sausage from scratch, grinding the pork and ingredients by hand into transparent skins. Every few inches they would twist the skins and tie them off with cord. Then the long line of sausages would be hung from horizontal bamboo poles rigged from the low ceiling in the back of the cellar near the wine barrels. In a week or so they were cured and ready to eat. They were very good but greasy, and tasted better when soaked in bubbling tomato sauce. When they were highly seasoned, which was often, I went for the Royal Crown. Sometimes they did liver sausage which was quite good. Less grease and more of a thick texture.

Adelina would also make macaroni from scratch.

Breaking eggs into a pile of dusty flour, she would knead it over and over, her thick arms churning the dough into a gooey pile. The rolling pin would flatten the dough into a long, thin sheet. Then, out came the harp. She would lay the flat dough over the top of the harp and push it through. Usually, there would be several sheets of dough to go through. When completed, she sprinkled the thin strands of dough with flour and let it sit for an hour or so, then she would drop the stiff strands into a boiling pot of water. Under a dim light, in a low-ceiling cellar, this old-world ritual would unfold. Quite a show for a five-year-old boy. Sometimes she would make tiny meatballs by the dozens, no larger than a marble, and sprinkle them over the macaroni and sauce.

Come to think of it, she cooked just about every day. In those days veal was cheap. She would buy it in thin strips and sauté it in olive oil and garlic. She then dipped it in a bread crumb and egg batter. The cutlets were paper thin and crispy, and were served with lemon slices. And never did Adelina's dark batter come off the cutlet. Never. I guess you could say in retrospect, "yes, Adelina was a pretty darn good cook." The aforementioned peppers and scrambled eggs were great except when she added the chicken livers. But the last straw was when she served boiled chicken. On those nights I headed for the hills.

Words & Music

*"The Italian music instantly takes me back to another time and place...
when I hit that button I am in contact with my family."*

One night in 1999 after a late movie I encountered a young, black "rapper" in the men's room of the Loews -White Marsh Theatre. Not more than 25, he was attired in jumbo pants and a football jersey with a baseball cap turned sideways. Inexplicably, Pavarotti's *Nessun Dorma* echoed over the P.A. system. As I picked up on the magic tones, the rapper began to bitch and moan about the crazy music. I couldn't help myself. I called him on it. His biggest complaint was the "crazy, foreign words." I looked him straight in the eye and said "Supply your own words and just let the melody wash over you." He remained silent for a moment then something clicked on, "Yeah," he said. "Yeah, yeah," and as Pavoratti was hitting the final notes, the rapper was seen walking out into the lobby "humming and jiving." Puccini would have smiled.

Almost every day I put on my Italian CDs, the louder the better. Operas, famous music and old-fashioned street songs. Seldom do I share this time with anyone else. My wife tolerates it in moderation and at much lower octaves. My sons laugh and tell me to turn it off. "You can put it back on when we leave." As classic as this music is it is becoming more and more obsolete, picking up no new advocates as the remaining faithful die off like clockwork.

Every year we go to an opera and it has become a staple in our Americanized family. Once a year, to get some culture. Why not. I am not a purist, but I can relate to the music and words of Italian opera and recognize the most prominent arias and some of the more obscure. Throughout America, the opera is struggling. Too much competition and too little time. Very few cities carry ethnic radio programming. For many years the Italian Hour on WCBM and WBMD, with Guy Sardella, and Mary Torierri played the Italian street melodies.

On more than one occasion I have been asked why I like that "old stuff." I just laugh and shrug it off. The Italian music instantly carries me back to another time and place to vivid remembrances of my youth, my family, and my heritage. I am the last link as my children and their children are totally American. As it should be. But when I hit that button I am in contact with my family. The memories flood in and the outside world is held at bay. It's that simple. It fills me with pride. Maybe that's why I'm more tolerant of neighbors' loud music than my wife.

During the War, the radio news was always on. The Italians under Mussolini were fighting for the Axis. It was a trying time for Italian-Americans. Obviously loyal to their new homeland, nevertheless they were concerned about Italy. They all respected Roosevelt and Churchill and hated Hitler and Tojo. But, when Mussolini came up there was a blind faith that was hard to shake, particularly for the immigrants. Italians have never been known as warlike people. In fact, they have been denigrated for their lack of "fighting spirit," their resolve always questioned. Italy had never been united since the fall of the Roman Empire. During major wars they were conscripted by paper mache governments to fight far-off battles. Italians would fight to their last breath to defend their own village but not someone else's village. During World War II the young Italian-Americans were full of piss and vinegar desperately trying to prove themselves and find a place of honor. The immigrant guys knew better. They were too crafty to spill their blood for just anybody.

Back in the 40's Grandpop Lolli liked to listen to the fights. All the Italians liked Joe Louis, whom they called "Joelooey" in one long syllable. Except of course when he faced Primo Carnera, Tony Galento, and Tami Mauriello, all stiffs, but nevertheless Italian. When Galento knocked Louis to the canvas our living room erupted with joy. Just a first- grader, I looked around in amazement at these full-grown men going bananas. It was short-lived as Louis got off the canvas and flattened Galento who trained on beer, dago red, and cigars.

Sicilian on my father's side and Abruzzesse on the other, I was caught in a vice not of my own choosing. It seemed like all my relatives looked upon me as "something special," the first of a new generation. "Speak English to Sonny." Yet, I was a poster child for Italia. At home, Adelina and Luigi spoke Italian to one another and broken English to me. My Sicilian grandparents seldom said a word to me. Grandma Mugavero would try but it all came out in Sicilian. Grandpa Gregory never said a word. My aunts, young ladies seeking upward mobility and the American Dream always spoke to me in English, but in Sicilian to their parents and a mixed bag to each other. Whenever emotions ran high Italian would take precedence. Uncle Marion spoke in monosyllables and pretty much ignored me.

Practically all the visitors to Hilton Street spoke Italian. By the time I was 10 years-old and developing my own persona I began to tune out the "old world diatribe." I never did speak the language but I was able to understand it very well and then respond in English. In addition, Italian music and radio programs were always on in the house. We also had an original collection of Caruso records which came out on special occasions. From an early age I took to them readily. The music made me feel good and also proud for some reason. For the most part, because of the music our house was a happy home.

La Musica

The more Italian music you know, the harder it is to pick a favorite. Music is a defining factor in being Italian. The works of Puccini have a lilt of paradise in every aria. Two of my favorites are: O' Sole Mio, which I have dubbed the Italian National Anthem, and Intermezzo by Mascagni from Cavalleria Rusticana, an instrumental where you can supply your own thoughts and words. I call this one the Italian Days of Our Lives. Italian music is better than the food and every opera has at least one defining aria that sweeps you away. Food satisfies the body, but music feeds the soul. Now, in my old age, I am strongly drawn to the obscure street songs, songs that I recall from childhood. Usually sung by Carlo Buti, and carried into the new millennium by Andrea Bocelli.

The Spirit of Little Italy

"...and now third and fourth generation immigrants live everywhere in Baltimore. It is the millennium and we are all Americans, as it should be."

Every major city has or has had its own "Little Italy," a community developed by the self-preservation instincts of the immigrants. Living and working together in common space, sharing the good and the bad times, gave these people a foothold in their new world. It also kept them segregated from the overall population and held back assimilation by decades. Most of Baltimore's Italians lived in Little Italy, a tiny neighborhood in East Baltimore, bordered by the Jones Falls to the west and Central Avenue on the east. Another Italian neighborhood was in the Lexington Market area on Eutaw Street and anchored by St. John's Church (now known as St. Jude Shrine). Most of the Italians there were *Cefalutans* from Sicily. Other than these two large enclaves, only smaller numbers of Italians were spread out all over town.

Italian immigrants were suited for manual labor and not much else. Many were farmers, stone masons, tailors, bakers, and fisherman, but, by-and-large, the pick and shovel was their coat of arms.

Many Italians who ended up in Baltimore came here seeking passage out west to dig for gold. Lack of funds, the great distance, loneliness and the Depression stopped their western migration. Baltimore's Italian population grew in leaps and bounds as the President Street Railroad Station was as far west as these Italians went. They settled in and around the harbor, an Italian Church was built and they began to try life on for size right here. Two of the biggest factors in the Italian assimilation into Baltimore were the Great Baltimore Fire in 1904 and the political rise of Little Italy boys Charles Palmisano and Tommy D'Alesandro. The fire devastated downtown Baltimore, literally burning it to the ground. In the ensuing decade, Italians were instrumental in rebuilding the city. The pick and shovel led them to municipal jobs and to the formation of numerous Italian construction companies. It gave these "unwelcome foreigners" a grub

The Great Baltimore Fire of 1904 devastated the city. Italian immigrants were among the first to join the rebuilding efforts and, over time, prospered through the birth of their own construction companies and trade businesses. At right, a first generation Italian, flanked by a fireman and two soldiers, survey the ruins of the Great Baltimore Fire. Note: City Hall in background.

stake in this city.

Charles Palmisano was one of the first elected Italian officials who began to use the "Italian vote" to get jobs and civic improvements for his paisanos. Tommy D'Alesandro carried it even further by becoming Mayor of Baltimore for four terms from 1947 to 1963. From that time on, Italians have made Baltimore a better place, for themselves and other minorities.

Today, the old neighborhood still stands. The gigantic Inner Harbor skyline looms all over her tired old houses. The population is aging. St. Leo's School has been closed since 1980. But the spirit of Little Italy still lives and breaths. Practically every Baltimore-born Italian still has some roots down there. The dozens of restaurants all tell a story. The church is packed every Sunday and the festivals are on-going.

By the time of the Great Depression, there were more Sicilians on the East Coast of America than there were in Sicily itself. These people from Southern Italy had nothing but the clothes on their backs. They were poor, uneducated, and lacking in skills. They were considered a huge burden. They banded together in eastern cities and began to eke out survival. Many Sicilians would go back home for seasonal work, sometimes staying away for several years, sending money back and forth. There was little work for them here. The Southern Italians were not candidates for assimilation. They spoke no English, lived together in ghettos, and shared a distrust for their American hosts. And the feeling was mutual. Though they were religious people, their spiritual zeal, then and even today, took on a pagan-like aura. Their ceremonies, ritualistic, loud and emotional, and always involving statues and pictures, evoked a superstition, poles apart from this nation's view of what Christianity was supposed to be. They faced an upward climb not too different from today's Johnny-come-latelys - the Koreans and Mexicans.

In the succeeding decade Italian labor gained a foothold through municipal jobs and construction crews. Even as common laborers, these little people gained a measure of "respetto" in their new country. Eventually, Italian construction companies formed.

Another piece to the puzzle was St. Leo's itself. The nerve center of Little Italy. The church and all it's close-knit family activities enhanced the quality of life for the second generation Italians who slowly had to cut the cord from their superstitious and ritualistic parents. If they were ever going to be Americans, this cord had to be cut. The church, with it's own "ancient values" somehow served as the jumping off point. And now the third and fourth generation of

these immigrants live everywhere in Baltimore, married to non-Italians as well. It is the millennium and we are all Americans, as it should be. Another big factor in the rise of the Italian-American was the Great Depression. The Italian immigrants were so poor and led such an austere life, that the Depression didn't really faze them. Their family unity and

St. Leo's Roman Catholic Church, the nerve center of Little Italy.

100

sense of community got them through and made them stronger.

St. Anthony at St. Leo's

In gratitude for being spared in 1904, the Italian population gathers each year on the closest Sunday to June 13, the feast of St. Anthony, to honor him for saving their homes. The St. Anthony Festival keeps bringing back Italian families from years past who have moved to the suburbs. The pull is strong as hundreds of Italians pray, party and eat as they walk the streets of their forebears on this occasion of recollection. In 1998, I attended this festival and was moved by the passion displayed there...

<u>Sunday, June 14, 1998...</u>

At 9:30 Mass, the church is packed. Close to 500 are in attendance. The old and infirm are transported up to the second floor by elevator. There is a mixture of young and old as a "seen better days" choir works to create a mood of prayer and reflection. Fr. Mike Salerno, the new Pallotine Order pastor from "Hell's Kitchen" in the "Big Apple" is already in gear. A dead ringer for a "mussed up Jerry Colonna," Fr. Mike delivers a serious message with a humorous ring, an Italian trait. Loud, soft, effusive and sad, he talks of the meaning of community. Of how sticking together and helping one another is not an outgrown myth. Of how Italians in this community continue to help each other make it. It is a lesson in civics, religion and goodwill. Loud and clear, with puns and jabs, always reaching out to young people. He closes by showing the new wall/alcove recently built to honor today's

101

guy – St. Anthony. He touches on St. Anthony's life of self-lessness and community service. By the time the choir hits the Catholic Communion hymn of Panis Angelicus (Bread of the Angels), you are feeling pretty close to God.

Fr. Mike has used all of his cards, saying parts of the Mass in Italian and encouraging responses from the congregation. The choir is now in concert and a steady stream of communicants make their way to the altar. Most are older. The history of Italians in our city is carved in their faces. They are life-long residents of this parish. Several generations of their families are here to pray and enjoy St. Anthony's Day. Especially today, you feel their prayers being heard. After Communion, the choir leads the congregation in an acapella rendition of The Lord's prayer that grabs you from within and holds you in an emotional vice.

All of these people feeling, believing, hoping and praying, and for a brief moment, they seem to melt into one.

There must be a St. Anthony up there. It sure as hell made you feel that way today.

Leaving Mass, we are urged to grab some consecrated

The Modern Spirit of Little Italy
The Lombardi Brothers pose with restaurateur and sportsman Naz Velleggia (2nd from right). All three Lombardis were standout high school athletes. (From left) Rick at Loyola, John at Towson Catholic and Chris at Towson High.

bread as a sign of faith. And a few seconds later, I am dipping it into a pot of fresh tomato sauce located in a festival booth on the street. Only in Little Italy. St. Anthony was working for me before I actually hit the street.

The Lodge

"The Italian ladies are weaving their way through the revelers, setting places and serving the salad."

I never grew up in Little Italy but the Mugaveros were an integral part of that scene since the turn of the century. As a child I was down there on Fawn Street almost every weekend. It made an indelible impression on me. The church, the streets and the people, people who walked, talked, and acted differently than folks in my neighborhood, intrigued me. There was no assimilation in Little Italy, whereas my West Baltimore neighborhood was a melting pot. From an early age I was always fascinated with "Little Italy," knowing my roots were there, always treating the place with a reverence yet always relieved to get back home. Through the years as a teenager I would run into Little Italy guys on the playing fields and in my uncle's corner store on Fawn and Exeter Streets. And whenever someone had a car we would end the night's activities eating in Little Italy. I was always keenly aware that this area never seemed to change. I always thought of my family whenever I'd get within a few blocks of the neighborhood. A neighborhood suspended in time.

Back in the late 80's I started a basketball breakfast to tip off the NCAA Tournament. It quickly grew in popularity and size. From a breakfast to a dinner. From a suburban diner to "The Little Italy Lodge." Paul Mugavero was truly returning to his roots. Every Friday night the Lodge members would cook an Italian dinner for their club members and friends. Informal on plastic dinnerware, the food is plentiful, hot, and deliciously Italian. The cost is so reasonably unreasonable, "The Italian Way," no one goes away hungry.

My event takes place on the Wednesday in March prior to the NCAA Tournament. The Lodge on 905 East Pratt Street is a low ceiling, one-story, cinder block building. Adjoining the St. Leo's School and Church Hall they have their own kitchen and can fit 275 to 300 people in for dinner. The Lodge members are older Italians mostly born and raised in Little Italy. They set up, cook, serve, and clean up after the Friday dinners and any catered events. The Lodge sponsors trips locally, regionally and abroad. The proceeds from their events help finance the cost for the active workers. And, they also have religious and cultural causes.

Naturally, everyone in this Lodge knows I am a Mugavero and not really a Baker. Many of them grew up in Little Italy with my family. The Lodge members go all out for my March Madness Dinner. The tables are set up in festive green and red linens, with wine on every table. As the assemblage gathers during the Happy Hour, you can see and feel the fellowship and good-natured bonding. The Italian ladies are weaving their way through the revelers, setting places and serving the salad. The meal is plain and simple Italian. Bread, salad, wine and plentiful amounts of spaghetti and meat balls are laced with basketball talk and fellowship. A collective buzz is in the air as people are having a good time. During the salad, guys are filling out their tournament brackets. Keith Mills of Channel 2 leads an invocation and makes appropriate introductions. Then some serious eating begins. I am too keyed up to eat, going over last minute details of my talk.

The ladies of the Little Italy Lodge serve pasta with style.

When I begin the program there is a set format but after 5 or 10 minutes the notes go out the window. I always worry about the ladies of the Lodge. The lights are dimmed and they are shadows in the background. But over the years I noticed that they always sat together listening attentively in the back. Because this event has always been traditionally "stag," their presence made me a bit nervous. When I approached a Lodge member about this dilemma he smiled and said, "Don't worry about it. It's nothing they haven't heard before and they enjoy the show."

I know my own father would have cringed and then some and my grandparents would have disowned me but that is the generation "slippage" that comes from living in America.

When the night is over Round 1 of the tournament has unfolded. This Dinner has become a part of the NCAA tournament for many Baltimoreans. Everyone has a wonderful time and their own reasons for attending. Without realizing it, the event takes us all back in time and suspends the present if only for a few hours.

Dinner Notes of Note

- Lodge President and head cook, Joe D'Adamo, in his apron and Terps hat, swearing in University of Maryland, Coach Gary Williams, as a honorary member of the Sons of Italy Lodge. His referring to Gary as Gaetano Guilliamere from the Federal Witness Protection Program, brought the house down.

- A little Italian octogenarian lady sidles up to me before the festivities begin and tells me how nice I look, but that on my best day, I could never measure up to my father's image.

- The guests devouring their spaghetti like it's their last meal.

- Jim Lacy being overwhelmed by the turnout of well-wishers on his Night.

- Paul Hoffman's family and friends posthumously accepting a portrait of "The Bear."

- Vince Bagli's annual appearance always as substantial as the meal.

- In Memorium to Coach Ray Mullis of Cardinal Gibbons.

- The rolling out of Charlie Eckman's biography by Fred Neil, "It's a Simple Game" and "Moments in Time" by yours truly.

- Honoring of Catholic League veteran coaches: Mark Amatucci, Gene Nieberlein, Dan Popera, Cokey Robertson and Gerry Savage.

106

Section III

"Il Crogiuolo"

The Melting Pot

Wonder Years

"Uncle Sam in a red, white and blue suit was always pointing a finger at us, and he looked pretty mean."

It was a cold and gray Sunday afternoon. We were playing dodge ball in the street. My father's voice summoned me into the house. The radio was blaring. The Japs just bombed Pearl Harbor. I was almost seven years old, but I still remember it clearly. December 7th has always been a day of reflection for me. For the nation and the world it was the beginning of an historic upheaval. For me it signaled the start of my youth.

Almost overnight I developed a global awareness. TV was non-existent, but newspapers, radio broadcasts, and *Life Magazine* were constants in our household. Dad was thirty-two, too old for the draft. My Uncle Marion was eighteen and joined the Coast Guard. We lived with my grandfather, who was "born on the other side." Every night we listened to the war news. Dad was a patriotic guy who admired Roosevelt, while grandpop still held an allegiance to "El Duce," whom I soon found out was Mussolini, the Italian dictator. Grandmom cried for the Italian soldiers stranded in Ethiopia and Mom worked in a tailor shop making Army uniforms.

After school I would listen to the old radio serials like Terry and the Pirates, Jack Armstrong, and the Shadow. The radio was our source of entertainment, drama, and news from the outside world. At night it was the ominous voices. Gabriel Heater, H.V. Kaltenborn, Walter Winchell and others had us riveted to the box. Every so often we would hear President Roosevelt and Prime Minister Churchill give speeches on some really important stuff. I hung on their words. I received a comprehensive geography lesson learning about places like Leyte, Guam, Wake Island, Corregidor, Luzon and Okinawa in the Pacific; Morocco, El Alamein, Tripoli, Libya and the Sahara in Africa; and Cherbourg, Bastogne, Normandy, Stalingrad and Potsdam in Europe.

Names like Patton, Montgomery, Clark, Basilone, Goering, Rommel, Eisenhower, MacArthur, Nimitz and Truman gave me a sense of drama and history. My career as a history teacher can be traced back to the news reels, papers, magazines and radio reports of the forties.

As time went by I began to notice changes. My dad became an Air Raid Warden. Every week our neighborhood had an air raid drill. For one hour after dark we would pull down the shades, turn the lights down very low and click off the radios. The Air Raid Wardens would walk around the neighborhoods with flash lights, checking every house. When the siren went off it was the signal to resume our normal lives. We had to be ready in the event the Japs or the Germans would bomb us. It was a very real feeling.

Silencing the Enemy

During World War II, in some Italian communities on the East and West coasts, the American Government confiscated the radios of unnaturalized Italian families, thinking they might be used as short wave radio signals to off shore submarines. The only submarines the Italians were associated with could be found in the kitchen and local food stores.

Throughout the community small flags appeared in the windows of some houses. The flag had a red border with a gold star inside a white background. Mom told me it meant the family had a person serving in the war.

When the War started I was too young to go into stores alone, but I began to realize that candy and other good stuff was becoming scarce. Rationing started in earnest. Grandmom showed me the ration stamp books every month. These books had pictures of meat, bags of sugar, and gas pumps. In order to buy these products, each family had to give up their allotted stamps plus the money. Fresh meat was a sometimes thing and a canned meat product, Spam, became a war time staple.

There were lots of ads in newspapers and on the sides of buses about buying War Bonds. Uncle Sam in a red, white and blue suit was always pointing a finger at us, and he looked pretty mean. Downtown on the corner of Baltimore and Charles Streets stood the Sunpapers building. From high up on the second floor came an electronic teletype with letters several feet high clicking out up-to-the-minute news into the darkened streets below. Standing on that corner waiting for the bus, reading news from around the world was heady stuff. People would cheer or quietly mutter.

By 1944 I had become a fanatical sports fan and partici-pant. The pictures in the papers and magazines had mag-netized the psyche of a young child. And, for the first time I saw sports icons Joe DiMaggio, Ted Williams, Hank Greenberg, Sammy Baugh, and Joe Louis on film in the MovieTone news, along with the unforgettable monotone of Lowell Thomas. On the home front, the Major Leagues were filled with old men, 4Fer's (exempt for medical reasons) and young kids. The product was watered down. I listened to the 1944 World Series between the St. Louis Cardinals and the St. Louis Browns, who ten years later would become the Baltimore Orioles. In 1945 it was the exciting series between the Detroit Tigers and the Chicago Cubs. I can still remember the starting lineups. Here in Baltimore, the 1944 Orioles

On December 2, 1944 (top right) I was nine-years old and went to Memorial Stadium in Baltimore, with my father, to see the Army-Navy football game. One of my biggest thrills that day was to see the parade of midshipmen and cadets (top left). Fifty-eight years later, the game and the "parade" (bottom right) returned to Baltimore and I attended once again — this time with my good friend Bill Hartleb (bottom left)... top two photos from Paulie Mugavero collection

won the International League title then beat the Louisville Colonels in the Little World Series. Over 52,000 viewed the final game in Baltimore.

The War also changed the college scene drastically. To avoid the common draft, college players opted for Officer's Training in the nation's V-12 programs. Thus the service academies corralled the nation's best players. The 1944 Army team won the National Title, going undefeated and beating Notre Dame 48-0. They repeated in 1945 and again routed the Irish 59-0. After the war in 1946, when all the athletes returned home to their original schools, they played to a 0-0 tie in Yankee Stadium.

In 1944, Dad took me to Baltimore Stadium to see the Army-Navy game. It was a bitter cold Saturday as the Midshipmen and Corps of Cadets marched down 33rd Street and into the wooden horseshoe that was Baltimore Stadium. The game admittance required the purchase of a U.S. War Bond and tickets were impossible to come by. Dad knew a fellow railroad man who was working a far gate, and in we went. Army had Blanchard and Davis, Mr. Inside and Mr. Outside. Both went on to win the Heisman Trophy. Navy also had a raft of stars led by Clyde "Smackover" Scott from Smackover, Arkansas. In a tough game, Navy died hard – 23-7. Fifty-eight years and thousands of sporting events later, the thrill of the 1944 Army-Navy game remains fixed in my memory.

The War news was getting better and better. Adults were upbeat. The end was near. The corner grocery began to carry "candy bars." I had never seen a candy bar. All I ever got was "penny candy," sold loose for one and two cents a piece. Because of the ration system, candy bars were sent

113

abroad to our troops, but all of a sudden in 1945, a little kid bought a Milky Way Bar and an ice cold Coke for a dime. Grandpop got a new car, Dad and Mom started going out to "night clubs" and Grandmom stopped crying over the Italian boys in Ethiopia. The war was ending and we were winning.

On VJ (Victory over Japan) Day I stayed up all night and roller skated around the neighborhood as people celebrated on their front porches and car horns honked incessantly into the wee hours.

Four years prior, when my father called me into the house I was a child. By VJ Day in 1945, I had become a young man. The War Years absorbed me and filled my senses with hundreds of experiences.

What a classroom. These were my "Wonder Years."

Going to Games

"My father told me that Di Maggio's family were Sicilian immigrants who became fishermen in San Francisco."'

After the War, people loosened up. Everyone seemed happy. Stores had new merchandise. You could buy candy bars, heretofore unknown to a 10-year-old, and ice cold sodas were only a dime. The Orioles began to play in the stadium on 33rd Street after old Oriole Park burned down in 1944.

But the events of that summer I will never forget are the trips to Griffith Stadium in Washington, D.C. to see major league baseball. My father had a good job as a clerk for the Pennsylvania Railroad and one of the perks of his job was free passage on the trains. The next few summers we went to D.C. on a regular basis. The major league rosters began to reclaim the stars who served in the Armed Forces. In addition to the exciting train ride, Dad always had good seats, close to the field. The first time I saw Joe DiMaggio, time seemed to stand still. As he stood in the batter's box with the bat in repose on his shoulder, you sensed that he was different as he dug in his cleats, took that wide stance, and stood motionless. He let a few high hard ones go by without flinching. Then, lifting his bat slightly off his shoulder he glared at the pitcher and waited. The fast ball came in as Joe flicked his hands through the hitting area. In a flash, the ball flew out of the park. The left fielder didn't move a muscle and Joe was rounding second before the people reacted to what they had just seen. A bolt of lighting in the early summer night. He rounded the bases with a loping grace. One that I observed 10 years later in our own Al Kaline. Di Maggio was special. He ran down fly balls with ease, and his body language set him apart. My father told me that Di Maggio's family were Sicilian immigrants who became fishermen in San Francisco and that he had two brothers who were also big leaguers.

Some other players I saw that summer were Hank Greenberg of the Detroit Tigers who had hit 58 home runs in 1938 and made the Hall of Fame, and the great Ted Williams who must have hit 20 straight line drives in batting practice. He was so skinny his uniform hung from his body as if he were a scarecrow. Bob Feller's fast ball made a loud popping noise like a firecracker. All the while we feasted on the best hot dogs I ever ate. They came in a transparent wax paper bag with "Briggs Sausages" written in big letters. My father only let me eat two each game. I could have eaten more. I would take the cardboard score card and keep a record of the game. The memory of these events would remain fresh in my mind for weeks. In those days there was no television to cloud reality.

Every year, the Variety Club put on a Redskins exhibition game in the stadium. I remember the Green Bay Packers and the Detroit Lions and of course the famous Redskins Marching Band with the Indian Drum Major in full tribal regalia. On our way over from West Baltimore, Dad would stop at Nate's and Leon's Delicatessen at North and Linden Avenues to get us lean corned beef sandwiches. It was hard to talk about the games at school in 1944 because most of my classmates had never seen a game, or knew they existed. So it became my secret.

The only negatives associated with these great experiences, was when I "talked to strangers." Invariably, I would comment or cheer during the games, much to the agitation of my father. Whenever I spoke out to anyone, I got a subtle poke or pull. Never talk to strangers was a phrase spoken often in my house.

The Paper Boy

"Hooper never left a fist fight a loser. He either won outright or left unbowed, getting the last word in as he spit blood. He was a proud little banty rooster."

When the War ended I was 10 and curious. Across the street lived Jimmy Hooper, a tiny, wise-cracking teenage rabble-rouser. Even though his name was Hooper, he was Italian as far as I could see.

He lived with his mother, grandmother and Uncle Tony, who was the Bellman at the Lord Baltimore Hotel. Their name was Janney, a derivative of Giannini and Italian was spoken in their home. According to Jimmy, Anna was related to A.P. Giannini, founder of the Bank of America in San Francisco, one of the wealthiest Italian businessmen in America. Anna would quote her grandfather who used to say "they are the rich ones, we are the happy ones." Anna, estranged from her Irish husband was old friends with my mom. She had a husky voice from chain smoking and wore too much lipstick. She was pretty, slender and laughed like a drunken sailor. And boy, did she love her Jimmy.

Hooper drove his mother crazy and always teased her. In fact, he was an expert at getting everybody's goat. He always bragged to the "dagos" about his Irish lineage, but woe to anyone who questioned him about being Italian. He always had it both ways. Hooper was small for his age, with coal black hair and eyes to match. He had no shot of being a high school athlete. Besides, there were more important worlds for him to conquer. Hooper was brilliant but hid it behind his own picket fence.

It was 1945 when I became Hooper's official "helper" on

His name may have been (Jimmy) Hooper, but his heart was Italian. Often, while waiting for the papers to arrive, we played catch in the street with a stuffed football... Paulie Mugavero collection

his Baltimore News Post paper route. I was in the fifth grade and he was a freshman at Mount Saint Joe. For the next couple years he was my role model for better or worse. Hooper actually had a double route, one that stretched from Hilton Street through the small arteries of Elbert and Morley Streets, onto Caton Avenue and up through Culver and Kossuth Streets to Old Frederick Road. Around 3:00 o'clock the paper truck unloaded the papers wired in bundles of around 250 on the corners of Phelps Lane and Hilton Street. Further up the route on North Caton Avenue was Hooper's other drop. Equipped with wire cutters, a thick paper strap and me, Hooper would lift the papers onto the bottom of the strap and, walking like a very pregnant woman, would work his way up Hilton Street. I would be sent up the little side streets and to out of the way houses, as Hooper worked the main drag.

I didn't do that much. I think he had me along for the company. Hooper liked to talk and tease. Talk and tease. He would tell me about all his female conquests and the ones to come. At the halfway point Hooper was always good for a soda or candy bar. We talked football. He loved "the Fighting Irish" of Notre Dame and boy, did he ever emulate them. Practically everyday his big mouth got him into some kind of jackpot. From a shouting match with a toothless grandmother over her paper being late or getting wet to a full-fledged, two-fisted battle in the middle of the street, usually with someone a head taller. I would always be scared and rooting for Hooper not to get killed while I picked up the scattered papers. Somehow, the papers got delivered. It would be dark when we hit Doc Kelly's Pharmacy on Old Frederick Road. Hooper loved the milk shakes and I drank

Cherry Cokes as we talked football. I got an education serving papers with Hooper. He had an opinion on everything. He was my conduit to the outside world. I was too young to hang around with him and the only time he had for me was when we were "on the route." Subconsciously, I savored my time with him. During the 1944-45 seasons we collected football pictures. Not only from the News and The Sun but from out of town papers purchased from the famous kiosk newsstand at Baltimore and Park Avenues. We both amassed huge scrapbooks and had a rivalry going over which of us had the most pictures. We had action shots from such faraway places as the Des Moines Iowa Register, the Los Angeles Chronicle, and the Minneapolis Times Dispatch.

Hooper was a tiny, little guy from a dysfunctional family, before they named them that. He worked the paper route and developed his own "weapons for success" as he encountered and overcame the human equation. Hooper never left a fist fight a loser. He either won outright or left unbowed, getting the last word, as he spit blood. He was a proud little banty rooster. As Irish or Italian as the circumstances warranted.

By the time I was 14 he was gone. Out of my life forever. I often wonder if Hooper ever knew that I made the St. Joe football team, and would he have cared. He received a Combat Citation in the Korean War. That figures. Years later I found out that Hooper became a doctor.

Eating American

"The "Hipp" was a grand theatre that enthralled you with its huge rounded ceilings, scalloped walls and larger than life tapestries. When the full orchestra revved up, the Hippodrome was its own Land of Oz."

Spending time traveling between Little Italy, ("Grandmom Downtown"), and our West Baltimore home on Hilton Street, I became familiar with Baltimore landmarks and different foods. On the corner of Fayette and Howard was the famous Nedick's chain from New York. Their grilled Coney Island hot dogs on soft buns with brown mustard were a classic. The orange drink served in long, thin logo glasses was a little pulpy, but cold and refreshing. It wasn't easy to get inside their doors on a Saturday. You were in the wheelhouse of a fanatical shopping bazaar. Wall to wall people. I was always attracted to the Howard Street side where a little guy with a Dead End Kid hat held forth, selling snacks and newspapers out of a makeshift kiosk.

Up and down Baltimore Street were several Little Tavern shops, the home of the 10-cent hamburger. Their motto, "Buy 'Em By The Bag." Grilled with a pickle and chopped onions, you could eat them like peanuts. Life's passing parade came through the doors of the Little Taverns. Hobos, ladies of the night, working stiffs, and even Alex Brown types were there to pick up a bag and a drink. Little Taverns have become extinct, except for a few spots in the

Downtown Baltimore right after the War. Trolley on Lexington Street turning down Park Avenue. Note Keith's theater and Reads Drug Store. Current site of Charles Center. Planters Peanut Store is just behind the trolley.

area. I'll say no more.

When my Dad took me to football games at Memorial Stadium, we always stopped at Nate & Leon's, located at the huge intersection of North and Linden Avenues. Their corned beef on rye with mustard was better than the game. I can still smell the steaming corned beef as the heat of the bag warmed my entire lap.

When shopping with my Mom, usually on a Saturday, we would have lunch at Reads Drug Store on the corner of Fayette and Lexington. Our favorite was hot vegetable soup with bacon, lettuce and tomato sandwiches on toast. The Lexington Street corridor from Charles Street west to Howard Street was a narrow 20th Century bazaar-like thoroughfare. In a two block area were four movie houses (Century, Valencia, Keith's, and the New). Across from the Keith's was the Planter's Peanut store with the replica of Mr. Peanut in top hat and cane. Mr. Peanut was the brain storm of an

Italian immigrant – Amedeo Obici. You couldn't walk past that store without being drawn in by the warm aroma of roasting nuts. And there was always the mounted policeman. The streets were filled with shoppers. The War was over and people were out in droves.

One Saturday, as Mom was trying on pair after pair of shoes in Wyman's Shoes, directly across from the Century, I sat there eating fudge out of her shopping bag and listening to, of all things, an NBC broadcast of the Michigan vs. Minnesota football game for the Little Brown Jug. Fritz Crisler versus Bernie Bierman. Was this great or what? I was all of ten-years-old.

Around the corner on Eutaw between Fayette and Baltimore, was the famous Hippodrome Theater. In addition to first-run movies of the day, they had a live stage show. Many of the great and near-great of the 30's and 40's performed on her stage. My most memorable moment was the appearance of Abbott and Costello. A bonus was the candy shop on the Baltimore Street side of the theater. They made fresh, hot caramel popcorn hourly. When I was ten, I got on the #20 bus in front of my house and in twenty minutes I would fly out the exit door at Eutaw and Baltimore Streets into the "Hipp" for the movie, stage show and hot popcorn. Total cost was 75-cents. The "Hipp" was a grand theatre that enthralled you with its rounded ceilings,

Hippodrome Stars

In the years between vaudeville and television, the Hippodrome was home to great numbers of live performers. Among those to grace the Hippodrome stage were:
Red Skelton
The Andrew Sisters
Ronald Reagan
Susan Hayward
Ann Southern
Gene Krupa
Edgar Bergen and
Charlie McCarthy

scalloped walls and larger than life tapestries. When the full orchestra revved up, the Hippodrome was its own "Land of Oz."

A few years later, we skipped Sunday Mass and went downtown to the New to see Richard Burton in the biblical epic, "The Robe." It was so awe inspiring and overpowering that I was feeling very guilty about missing Mass. So, as soon as Richard Burton was converted on the screen, we headed for the Basilica on Cathedral Street to catch the late afternoon Mass and a little redemption.

When our family would drive back home from Little Italy, dad would often stop at a little "greasy spoon" bar and grill on East Pratt Street called Tolson's. He would run in quickly and

A view of the Hippodrome stage from the side. The theatre was so ornate it resembled a painting... it was a 10-year old's paradise.

come back out with a steaming bag of fresh, home made crab cakes to die for. And just around the corner from Fawn Street was Lombard Street with her Corn Beef Row, where you got a hot, lean corn beef on rye for 35 cents.

On summer vacations to Wildwood, New Jersey, we would eat Taylor Pork Roll sandwiches. They had shops all along the Jersey shore. Eventually, Taylor Pork Roll showed up in super markets and is still around today. Sliced thick and grilled on a warm bun, they were a delicacy.

At home during the summer, the smell of crabs and Old Bay seasoning came through our neighborhood every night. Benkert's Park, an old German beer garden, was just a block away. It was owned by the Benkert family whose children Buzzy, George, Mickey and Mary Ellen were my classmates at St. Joseph's Monastery. Throughout the summer we would order crabs, hot roast beef sandwiches, sour beef, shrimp, and crab cakes. Running across Caton Avenue with a five spot in my hands, I was in Heaven.

Because of my "worldly experiences" I got to know about food beyond Adelina's kitchen. I craved all that "American Stuff" over the force-fed Italian menu of my grandparents. I was growing up American. It was not until I grew much older that I began to appreciate "La Cucina Italiano."

The Veiled Terrors

"Every Sunday we attended the 9:00 a.m. Children's Mass, sitting in assigned pews by class. If you could not attend for a legitimate reason, you presented your teacher a sealed, written note from your parents, which was recorded in a black book. Then all week you were eyed scornfully."

In Little Italy there were Italian nuns who nurtured the kids and kept them protected from prejudice. At St. Joseph's Monastery Church and Grade School, in Southwest Baltimore, we were educated by the School Sisters of Notre Dame and led to salvation by the Passionist Fathers of Union City, New Jersey. A powerful combination. The school and convent were separated from two large churches by a huge expanse of ground called "The Grove," that was squarely framed by a nine foot page fence between Frederick Avenue and Old Frederick Road. The overall area encompassed over 25 acres. This feudal refuge and several cemeteries were squarely in the middle of an old-fashioned row house neighborhood.

The nuns and priests worked together for our spiritual well-being. Every Sunday we attended the 9:00 a.m. Children's' Mass, sitting in assigned pews by class. If you could not attend for a legitimate reason, you presented your teacher a sealed, written note from your parents, which was recorded in a black book. Then, all week you were eyed scornfully. Woe to the child who missed two Sundays in a row. Although we received a solid primer education, Religion was the focal point. We made our Communion in the first grade, followed by Confirmation in fourth or fifth grade. Every week we were marched up Old Frederick Road for Confession, usually on a Friday morning. During Lent you were expected to attend Mass in the mornings. Many students became Altar Boys to assist the large population of priests in the saying of Mass. Girls sang in the choir and were always seen at Novenas and Benedictions with their parents.

The nuns were severe in their quest for "law and order." They seemed to favor the girls. There was little patience with the slow and the lazy. They would publicly blister a child for anything, academic or personal. Woe to the child who came to school with sleep in their eyes, or an unkempt appearance.

In the fourth grade we had a rather old, weather-beaten nun named Sister Agneta. She was overdue for the rest home by several years. We didn't learn much that year. She loved to slap kids around. In this class we had one out-of-

The nuns of St. Joseph's Monastery, who could intimidate any kid with a single menacing glance, oversee the daily Pledge of Allegiance. In the upper right is Pop Maranto's Confectionery Store.

place youngster. His name was Dominic Machetti, and he was older, overweight, and underachieving. He lived on Lohrs Lane off Frederick Avenue in a neighborhood called "Checkerboard Hill." Even in the Forties there were Blacks in our neighborhood. Dominic was raised by his grandmother. He lived in a dysfunctional house with older cousins. He was always a late arrival, having spent half the night hanging around the dice games on the Hill. A 10:00 o'clock scholar. When he opened the classroom door, a hush would come over the class. As Dominic would mutter his half-hearted excuses, Sister Agneta would blister him before he was relegated to the back of the room, to continue his siesta. Being one of the few Italians in our class, I was always worried how Dominic's persona reflected on us as Italians. He was big for his age and a fish out of water. On this particular day, Agneta had her fill. As Dominic entered, you could smell the street on him. Agneta got right in his face, breathed the nicotine then began to scold him, like a Marine drill sergeant. Poking his stoic countenance, she ordered him to empty his pockets. When the cigarettes appeared (Pall-Mall's as I recall), she crossed the line, slapping the poor kid across the face and calling him "a dirty Italian." Showing no emotion, Dominic grabbed up his smokes and did an about face out the door, never to return.

For eight years we were taught by these "veiled terrors." Spelling, penmanship, music and arithmetic were drilled into our heads. The music was for the Masses, Benedictions, and religious services. The most explosive days were the Math classes at the blackboard. Four to six students would take their long division homework up to the board under the watchful eyes of the nun. Woe to the one with the wrong answer. I always enjoyed the morality play as it unfolded before me. Up at the board, the nervous, uncertain kids would write in a halting fashion, constantly shifting their eyes, not their heads, to the "smart ones" who were proudly making their chalk sing. If the nun was in a bad mood, there would be trouble. These long division sessions always ended up with physical confrontation. A yardstick/pointer poke or the occasional smacking of the head on the blackboard. When a yardstick blow to baggy corduroys softened the whack, the nun would then change her attack to jabs, slaps and pokes to the body.

One day, poor Gerard Hudzik's head print stayed on the board all day, thanks to his Bryl Creme-soaked dome. On some occasions, these confrontations would become so comical that one of us would burst out laughing in our seats. This "insubordination" was met with a counter attack. The nuns would get their satisfaction and the blackboard kids would get relief. Math days were always fun, as long as you weren't called.

Several times a year, we were expected to sell chance books for the Parish coffers and an accounting was held daily at the blackboard or on a chart. In the middle of the drive, the nuns would do a "roll call," praising the leaders and urging the shirkers to "get on the board." We also had to save up pennies for the "Chinese Babies" being brought into Catholicism. So many dollars converted into so many "saved babies." The entire school was held accountable for the number of pagan babies we would deliver into Christianity. In the summer, the Parish held a Carnival. The nuns were usually on vacation or religious retreats, but every now and then, those black robes would appear, and whatever you were doing at the moment would stop. Your posture would straighten and your voice would modulate. No doubt, the "veiled terrors" had influence, even on a warm summer night in July.

The most embarrassing time was Report Card Day. Four times a year, this "day of reckoning" would arrive. The door would knock as the nun proudly opened it. One of the Passionist Fathers would enter to a collective, "Good Morning, Father." Unfurling his black cape with the Passionist logo/crest, he would acknowledge us to be seated. The nun would move to the periphery of the room. Father Leo would crack a few corny jokes then, holding the report cards in both hands, would begin to give the "roll call."

Starting with the best to worst, he would call out the names, meting out praise to the A's. From the periphery, the nun would gauge the demeanor and manners of each child as they would come up to the front desk to receive their report card. Woe to anyone who walked up too slowly, or acted in a manner to show a lack of respect. The cards had to be taken home, signed by the parents, and then returned in a few days. In addition to the grades A through F with plus or minus signs, there were grades for Attitude, Effort, and Conduct, plus absence and lateness figures. This day of reckoning placed everyone under a microscope and into an exact "pecking order." As the passing parade unfolded, you could see a pattern. The A students were dressed better, were neater and cleaner, and displayed perfect manners. As the parade continued down the pecking order, the kids became more unkempt, less confident and subject to the priest's admonishments to do better. A Sociology lesson I never forgot. By the time he got to the last few kids, an awkward tension evolved. In that classroom you were on pins and needles, waiting for your name to be called. Living outside Little Italy, Italians had no cushion. You grew up faster and were assimilating into American life quicker, for better or for worse.

The Altar Boy

"The harder I tugged the more the stand stood still. Finally I gave a hard upward pull. The lights flickered and glass clicked as the vigil light stand lurched over onto me."

Because the Monastery was home to dozens of ordained Passionist priests waiting to be assigned to their global missionary assignments, we had Mass every day. Not only on the main altar, but the two side altars and small alcoves on each side of the huge church. During Lent, at 7:00 a.m., there were as many as nine Masses going on in one church attended by several hundred people. In the cold church enveloped by incense candles, one felt a spirituality of mind and body. In retrospect it was probable that no such religious scene had ever been equalled or repeated in all of Christendom, ever. Adelina loved the Monastery church, often saying it reminded her of the churches in Italy.

To serve the myriad of Masses and other services, the St. Joseph's Monastery School provided trained Altar Boys. Fr. Leo Vanston was in charge of the recruitment and training of these "angels in waiting." In addition to the Masses there were evening benedictions, weddings, baptisms, May processions and funerals. All needing live bodies trained in the nuances of the service. Father Leo maintained a standing army of fifty or so grammar school students. Some stayed all the way through high school. Training started with the learning of the Latin prayer responses and the various bodies of the Mass. The rookies started in the sixth grade. Every Friday after school we would meet in a musty locker room in the basement of the church sacristy. A training session would be followed by the week's assignments. After a year or so you began to get the coveted jobs, Sunday Masses and weddings where you could get a tip from the bride and groom. The altar boys room had metal lockers filled with ankle length red or black cassocks buttoned from ankle to neck. Starched white surplices slipped over top of the cassock. There were dozens of sizes available. Father Leo expected his altar boys to be fitted well. Shoes shined and fresh haircuts were a given. And, woe to the young man who showed up with sleep in his eyes. You were expected to give the prayer responses in Latin in a quick and timely fashion, not letting the priest have to wait. Father Leo always got a scouting report from the other priests.

The Passionists

The St. Joseph's Monastery School and Churches were owned and operated by the Passionist Fathers of Union City, New Jersey. They were not local secular priests. Their stock in trade was Missionary work, not only in the poor areas of America but throughout the world.

During their heyday, the Monastery housed over two dozen ordained Passionists. The parish was administered by several older priests who conducted religious services that attracted people from all over the city and adjoining states. They raked in lots of cabbage in those days.

Being an altar boy at the Monastery was a serious commitment. One of the perks was that the nuns seemed to give you a break. That "old benefit of the doubt" in grading evaluations and their reticence in administering corporal punishment to one so close to the Altar of God, came in handy. Some of the less committed used their privilege to eat the unconsecreated hosts and wash it down with chilled altar wine for their early morning breakfast. Remember, there were no 7-11's in those days. Perhaps HE will take that into consideration.

One of my most memorable moments as a page of the Lord came at the 11:30 Mass on a Sunday during Lent. I was a thirteen year old

The Altar Boys of St. Joseph's Monastery, circa 1952. Fr. Adrion Poletti, Pastor with Archbishop Shehan. Note: Fr. Albert Catanzaro is pictured in the upper center.

seventh grader. At the Communion rail were two large wrought iron vigil light stands holding at least 100 votive candles. Before Mass the parishioners would come up to the altar rail, light a candle and say a brief prayer for special intentions. The stand was heavy and unwieldy with four swivel wheels allowing it to roll back and forward. Prior to Holy Communion it was the altar boys job to wheel the stand back from the rail. The church was packed. Music and incense filled the air. It was my first "big time" assignment. All the early morning assignments on the side altars on week days had paid off. I was now on in prime time. As I moved down to the Communion rail, I suddenly became a little nervous. Never having to move the stand before, I was surprised by its weight and bulk. The wheels were inverted, and no one told me about the iron foot brakes that kept the wheels immobilized. The urgency of the Communion hymn put me in a panic. The harder I tugged the more the stand stood still. Finally I gave a hard upward pull. The lights flickered and glass clicked as the vigil light stand lurched over onto me. The crash reverberated throughout the huge church as the assemblage let a collective gasp. Laying there partially pinned down by this wrought iron monster, I struggled free and shed the burning surplice. I can still recall the heat pulsing through my reddened cheeks. This epiphany signaled an end to my career on the altar and put me back on the Nun's "hit list."

Serving on the altar was a big thing in those days. Several of our student body became Passionist priests. A few years later Father Leonard, who succeeded Father Leo, put it to Timmy Hodge point blank, "Altar boy or basketball, choose." He chose hoops and went on to play and graduate from Calvert Hall and Baltimore University.

Geppi

"For the next few years every kid in Irvington knew about, talked about, and wanted to be like Geppi."

Growing up in West Baltimore before television, kids searched for their own means of identity, expression and fun. Movies were a cheap thrill and opened up a window to the world. A world that was just emerging after the Great War. My outlets were the neighborhood playing fields and movie houses like the Edgewood on Edmondson Avenue, the Astor on Poplar Grove Street, and the beloved Irvington on Frederick Avenue just a block up the street from Mt. St. Joseph's High School.

On a fall Saturday afternoon in 1946 at the age of 11, riding my bike through Irvington, I had a dilemma. Go to see St. Joe play St. Paul's on Gibbons Field or see a John Wayne cowboy movie at the Irvington. With only a quarter in hand, there were financial considerations. I decided on a double feature. St. Joe first and John Wayne second. Mom was working a half day at the sweat shop and then she would go shopping. My dad was

Gibbons Field

Gibbons Field was named after the famous Cardinal Gibbons. When Cardinal Gibbons High School was opened in 1963, and became an athletic rival, St. Joe dropped the name, and the field became Ryken Field.

working his second job at the race track. I wouldn't be missed til at least 6:00 p.m.

Hiding my bike under a pile of leaves, I crab-walked the steep hill up to the Gibbons Field fence. There was always a uniformed Pinkerton guard but he had quite an area to police. Sometimes kids would climb the fence and simultaneously hop over and scatter much to the chagrin of the guard-turned-Keystone Kop.

This day I had to make it over or through the fence. I wasn't going to blow my only quarter on a ticket and forfeit John Wayne. Still too small to climb the fence I inched along the base, found a soft spot, scraped away some leaves, got

John Geppi left many would-be tacklers in his wake during his Mt. St. Joe career before moving on to Villanova, where he also dominated. (1947 vs. City @ Baltimore Stadium)

my head under the wire fence, and crawled my way through. The band was playing and the sun was shining as I ran into the safety of the crowd. The St. Joe team, in royal purple looked awesome. They could have been the Chicago Bears for all I knew. Other than black and white newsreel clips I had never seen football players so up close and personal. I took it all in, hooked forever. The Gaels were led by an unusual player. Small and compact, he ran all over and through poor St. Paul's. His name was John Geppi. For the next few years every kid in Irvington knew about, talked about, and wanted to be like Geppi. No posters, pictures or film clips, just the telling and re-telling of his latest accomplishments. He became a local legend. Icons usually don't have two names. This blazing, tiny fireball was simply Geppi. A sprint champion who shaped up at about five-foot-five, one-seventy, Geppi would either run by or over confounded opponents. Too small for Coach Vic Wojcihovski to send up to Notre Dame. Vic sent him to Villanova to play for his ex-Irish teammate, Jim Leonard. The "Gep" averaged 6.0 yards per carry and capped off his career with an 80-yard touchdown run in the Harbor Bowl at San Diego in 1950.

Geppi's father was a Sicilian immigrant who ran a successful fruit and produce business in Baltimore's Lexington Market where Geppi and his brothers ran the stalls and streets of West Baltimore. Geppi's brother Frank also starred at St. Joe. Later I came to find out the Geppi family, just like the Lolli's, also ran afoul of the infamous Lieutenant Emerson and his Vice Squad back in the 50's. As Geppi tells the story, he arrived back in Baltimore after his final exams at Villanova. Summoned immediately to work in the family office above their Lexington Market stall, he had no time to

141

even unpack before he was taking "action on the phone." As fate would have it that afternoon, Emerson's maul hammer pounded in the office door and his goons came thundering through. They whisked away everything on the desk, including Geppi's school books, into large evidence bags.

Soon after the Geppi's were brought up on charges. Lieutenant Emerson in his most bombastic, blowhard manner showed the judge exhibit A, a blue notebook filled with "secret coded" numbers. Proof of the bookmaking operation. Judge Anselm Sodaro sagely looked at the presented evidence, smacked the gavel and dismissed the case. Emerson's evidence proved to be Geppi's Villanova Trigonometry Blue Book Exam notes.

Watching Geppi play that afternoon defined reality for me. Later John Wayne paled in comparison. Nothing takes the place of a live performance. Especially if the performer is Italian.

Rocket

"People gravitated to Rocket. He was such a hard worker — a role model and a teacher."

Whenever I hear Elton John belt out his famed "Rocket Man," my mind races back in time. It's 1947, and Bob Leishear is alone on a hot summer morning at the P.S. #91 athletic field, casually known as "Behind the School." A solitary figure, he labors around the cinder track as the humid day unfolds. Quietly leaning on my two-wheeler, watching him sweat and work, I felt like an intruder. Spotting me, he nodded. I came closer. Into his space, into his world. He bore a nasty scar on his shin from knee to ankle and he didn't run that fast. Years later I learned this scar was the result of being hit by a car. The accident occurred on Baltimore Street near Abington Avenue, right by Uncle Arnold's barber shop, and Rocket was attended to by an off-duty fireman named "Reds" Duvall who set the leg and called an ambulance. In his day, Reds was also a talented multi-sport athlete. Rocket recounted this story to me as I introduced him to Herb Duvall, Reds' son, at a Mount St. Joe Hall of Fame dinner some fifty-five years later. And, Reds' youngest son, Dan, was an outstanding player for me at Towson Catholic in the sixties. Baltimore is truly a small town that belies its size — a city of neighborhoods.

Rocket, the All-American boy, as pictured in his 1947 Forest Park High School yearbook.

Back in those days, Rocket was always working and training. He was a star athlete at Forest Park High School in the late 40's. A triple threat football player. I think he was pretty fast when he was a kid. That's why they called him Rocket. I always associated his name with someone striving upwards to a higher goal, much like a rocket ship. For a twelve-year-old kid to know and interact with an older guy named Rocket was pretty cool.

Rocket carried a large duffel bag. Inside it were some things I had never seen before. A discus, two iron balls (eight and twelve pound shot puts), starting blocks and a ball and chain that looked like a Medieval torture device (hammer throw). In a canvas sheath, he carried a javelin and an aluminum vaulting pole. Rocket was a Decathlon athlete (ten grueling events). An event with Olympic tradition dating back to the ancient Greeks, with absolutely no Baltimore heritage. Rocket was a solitary figure, grinding and training long and hard in these backbreaking events. Being around him gave a young person the feeling that hard work was worth it. In the evenings, when the field was filled with neighborhood softball games, kids running all around, and the Italian men rolling a Bocci game, Rocket could be found in the far off reaches, pole vaulting or high jumping in a makeshift pit. He was a heroic figure. Handsome, with blondish-brown hair and light eyes, he had a large chest and slender legs, stood around six feet, at 165 pounds, with a healthy tan from all that Decathaloning in the sun.

As I got to know him, I became familiar with his workouts. I would retrieve his discus and shot puts, clock him in the 440, and help him pack up all his stuff. There were times when he had no transportation and he would leave his bag and poles in our yard, next to the fig tree. I would always make sure they were covered up. For a few short years while growing up, Rocket was my hero. A guy from another planet. He helped a lot of kids out with conditioning and techniques. Instead of pursuing formal education, Rocket studied Track and Field, absorbing hundreds of books on the subject. And, with his unrelenting practical application, he became an expert in the field. One of his "Behind the School" projects was Jimmy Franz, a short little dynamo who he developed into the Maryland Scholastic Association Shot Put and Discus Champion in 1951. A few years later another neighborhood prodigy, Tom Hatcherson, did the same at Poly. People gravitated to Rocket. He was such a hard worker – a role model and a teacher. I am convinced that Rocket Leishear, had he gone on to college, would have had a fantastic career and today would be sitting somewhere in a hallowed university's athletic center in a building that bears his name, a revered professor emeritus. However, it really doesn't matter because he is a man who took his passion to the limits of his personal capability and influenced many along the way.

He taught track and field techniques to all who came his way. In 1998, almost 50 years later, Rocket coached Ron Mellerson of Mt. St. Joe to the shot and discus titles that

Franz and Hatcherson had achieved in the 50's. Rocket also coached amateur football in the 50's and 60's when that sport was still alive.

In 1951, I was playing for Mt. St. Joe and we had a preseason scrimmage with the fabled Wildwood A.C., an amateur team made up of ex-high school and college players. I got a chance to make some good yardage. On one handoff, I shot through the hole, cut left, and ran untouched over the goal line. Behind the End Zone, wearing a gray sweatshirt and puffing on a cigar, was Rocket Leishear. I felt six feet tall.

Rocket is 73 years young. He still competes – winning the Senior and Super Senior Olympic field events. Throughout his life he coached and mentored hundreds of young people. Little did he know, his first one was me.

Dangerous Undertakings

"My family never knew about any of this stuff. I was an Italian from a responsible and loving family. One that cared and supposedly watched over me. They surely would have freaked."

When I was ten the bicycle enlarged my world. With dad working two jobs, my mom sewing away in the sweat shop, grandpop designing suits, and Adelina cooking up a storm and running the house, I was on my own. I knew every alley and side street in West Baltimore. Flying through the neighborhood on a skinny two wheeler gave you confidence and a feeling of invincibility. When I see those crazy skateboard and biker kids in the streets and on TV, a half century later, I can understand their mind set. Riding bikes took us to new worlds. Freedom with the wind blowing in your face was heady stuff.

At the end of Hilton Street was Carroll Station where local trains would pick up people on the way to New York and D.C. I remember standing on the platform area with hundreds of people when FDR died in 1945. We laid coins on the track to be picked up as souvenirs after his funeral train came by on the way to Hyde Park. I kept that mashed coin all through high school. I remember showing it to my fifth grade class.

Next to the passenger rails were train tracks where box cars loaded with freight, oil tankers and open coal cars sat. We would climb up the ladder which was at least chest high and wander all over the cars. Sometimes the box cars were open and in we would go. On the adjacent track the high speed passenger trains would whiz by so fast that your hair would stand straight up and the sweat would dry on your brow, all in an instant. It was a dangerous but exciting undertaking. One false move and you could be dead. When the freights started moving we jumped off pretty quick. The harsh sound of the couplings banging and the cars picking up speed was the final call.

◆

The Gwynns Falls, at the bottom of a deep gorge ran through our neighborhood. From north of the Edmondson Avenue bridge through a massive stone quarry past the West Baltimore Street bridge and train viaduct on down to today's harbor in Little Italy and out into the Patapsco River Drainage Basin. On Saturdays we usually went to the Astor Theatre, a tiny little dump on Poplar Grove Street off of Edmondson Avenue. We could cut through the Falls walking over the drainage pipes that spanned the falls, or go up Hilton Street to Edmondson Avenue then walk over the Edmondson Avenue bridge. Either way it was an adventure. Walking down the Falls through the woods you could see the Edmondson Avenue bridge looming above, some hundred or more feet. Looking down the Falls was the Baltimore Street bridge and viaduct about a mile away that supported the Pennsylvania Railroad trains that flew up and down the East Coast. The adjoining Baltimore Street Bridge signaled the last leg for the #20 bus that connected East and West Baltimore and all points in between.

We crossed the Falls by walking atop two large sewer pipes only a few feet apart. The pipes were 24-inch in circumference and the span at that juncture was several hundred feet. Although the pipes were only a few feet above the falls, after a strong rain the water was fast and ominous. Jagged rocks jutted out from the water. You had four ways to go "over the pipes." Tiptoe over one pipe, straddle both pipes and walk very slow, run across one pipe, or if you were "chicken," straddle one pipe and shimmy across on your butt. Guys decided based on the weather and their level of courage on that given day. One of our neighborhood kids, Jerry Kraft, drowned in the Falls around that time.

◆

The days we walked up and over the Edmondson Avenue bridge, were the most harrowing of all my youthful experiences. Leo Wenker was a year or so older and lived across the alley from me. He smoked, cussed and was totally fearless. The Edmondson Avenue bridge was around one hundred yards long. A busy thoroughfare for cars, trucks and the #14 trolley. The bridge did not have a conventional hand railing. Instead, pedestrians were protected from the falls below by a rounded concrete abutment, a good two to three feet thick. A kid had to

The Silver Meteor

Right before the War (1939) the Pennsylvania Railroad instituted express travel up and down the East Coast, the precursor to Amtrack and the bullet trains of Europe. Their pride and joy was the Silver Meteor that took passengers from New York to Florida, and several places in between in record time. Dad, who had just become a ticket clerk at Penn Station, was extremely proud of his job and particularly the Silver Meteor, seven stainless steel coaches decorated in a citrus motif of green, yellow and orange. A year before my "out of body" experience, Dad took me to New York and back in one day and later that year, he took the family to Florida on the fabled Silver Meteor.

149

get on his tip toes to look over into the falls below. Leo would jump up onto the abutment at the bridge's beginning and start to walk his way across the bridge. We would beg him to come down, but he would keep going. I always worried about a strong wind or a beeping car, but he was oblivious. Eventually he would jump down and join us, especially if a lit cigarette from a passing vehicle hit the curb. "Butt trapping" was a macho thing in those days. Leo was a real dead-end kid. His secret: he always walked on the inside edge.

◆

One summer we somehow got into the habit of "jumping coal trucks." We would wait on the corner of Hilton and Baltimore Streets. One day three of us got on top of one truck headed north. For the first few miles we were "riding high" and so proud of ourselves. Then the whirling coal dust and slag began to blow all over us. Eventually we were discovered and run off the truck by a very mad, cursing driver. By this time we were in Hanover, PA. Penniless and covered head to foot in a coat of dust, with night descending. An old man in a country store let us wash up, gave us each a soda and drove us back as far as Reisterstown Road, where we hitch hiked back. It was 1947 and I was still young enough to get whacked and punished.

◆

Leo also took us under the Baltimore Street Railroad viaduct. A concrete bridge about a mile above Carroll Station. Imposing, it looks like the ancient Roman Viaduct bridges depicted in the history books.

On the rounded arches beneath the span that supported the bridge, were imbedded iron grippers every two feet. It was cold and clammy inside the viaduct as sunlight never

Climbing along the arched underbelly of the Baltimore Street Viaduct, nearly 100-feet above the Falls, was among the most dangerous of childhood undertakings. Note: The Baltimore Street Bridge is on the far right. Baltimore Street ends about one-mile up the hill.

shone in there. At its highest point, the viaduct was nearly 100-feet above the Falls. When the Pennsy's Silver Meteor whipped over the tracks above, the vibrating noise was enough to chill your bones. The whole trip took about thirty minutes of painstaking hand over hand climbing to go no more than a hundred yards. Once you started there was no turning back. I will always remember Leo saying, "Don't look down." I heeded the word of experience. Coming over the downside of the arch was even more harrowing as you were climbing down backwards. At the end of the span we had to hang and jump about ten feet to the ground below. Several homeless bums sitting on their knapsacks looked at us in astonishment. A truly dangerous undertaking that I did only once. It was as close to an out of body experience as any kid could have. I never told anybody. In the succeeding years when I rode the #20 bus down to Little Italy and passed over the bridge, looking at the viaduct, I would get an eerie feeling. For an eleven-year-old it was Mount Everest. I added Italian guilt to my fear when I realized that as part of his job my father would be selling tickets to that very train that was whizzing over me. That night at the dinner table Dad asked me how my day was, like he knew something was up. I quickly concocted a mundane story then added, "Dad, I heard, I mean I saw, The Silver Meteor go by the neighborhood today." He looked up from behind the newspaper and smiled. He seemed pleased. Dad loved the Silver Meteor.

◆

When going to the Irvington Theater from Hilton Street we would invariably cut through the New Cathedral Cemetery. There was a gate at the junction of Monastery and St. Joseph's Streets. Ignoring the No Trespassing sign, we would climb the fence. Leo spotted an open manhole cover. Of course he climbed down, around ten feet. The same iron grippers were in place. We found out that you could stand up down there. The underground drain was about five feet high and slanted upwards. You could see snippets of light at intervals up the tunnel when sunlight would break through the drainage grills. Leo climbed out, ran over to the corner grocery store and came back with a handful of old newspapers. Rolling one up as a torch, he lit it with his butane lighter and proclaimed, "Follow me." We started out brave and cocky, following Leo's

Adelina's Holy Card

yellow flicker ever upward. A few rats appeared and disappeared as the tunnel became damp and dripped with smelly water. The tunnel began to take an upward slant. Past the half way point Leo ran out of newspaper, but he kept his lighter working and we followed the shards of sun light. We had traveled the width of the New Cathedral Cemetery, at least one mile, where the drain reached an abrupt end. Leo climbed the iron grippers and put his shoulder to the man hole cover to no avail. We began to scream and yell and Leo pounded his lighter on the man hole cover. In a few minutes several grave diggers took a pick to the cover and dislodged it from the grit and rust covered rim. Climbing out of that tunnel into broad daylight we scattered before the cemetery people could decide what to do with us.

My family never knew about any of this stuff. I was an Italian from a responsible and loving family. One that cared and supposedly watched over me. They surely would have freaked. They had no idea, but maybe that's why Adelina always had the Holy Card with the Guardian Angel looking over the children on her dresser.

Ronnie

"The fight carried on for a long time. There were no clinches, wrestling or scuffling. It was just him, and me avoiding the bombs, then counter-punching as the crowd closed in on us. The fight and the ring of spectators moved all the way around the school."

Growing up, I had more than my share of scrapes and scuffles. Being a tiny ethnic kid with a lot to say made me a target. I never picked on anyone and seldom backed down, but I was always aware of the odds. Usually the underdog, I had my share of black eyes and split lips.

One day, at the old PS #71 School grounds, I got into a squeeze I could not avoid. Located on Old Frederick Road between the Monastery Church and New Cathedral Cemetery, #71 had a dirt playground with several softball diamonds crammed into a few acres. The bases were permanent concrete blocks embedded into the dirt. According to my mom, they were put in by the old WPA work details. There was a small playground and a basketball court. The neighborhood kids skated and rode their bikes in and around the pathways surrounding the school. On a muggy summer evening, the fields and paths were abuzz with activity. On these nights, it was easy to reflect on Baltimore neighborhoods and their penchant to "cool off." Snowballs must have become the law of natural selection/evolution that hatched itself from the town's unending humidity. Sugar flavored juice and shaved ice in a cup for a nickel was magic.

This night in the Summer of 1949, I was coaching the Megary Midget girls' softball team. Mrs. Megary was our Cub Scout Leader and neighborhood organizer. She asked me to coach the team even though these girls were my peers. I did the best I could, teaching them the fundamentals that I knew. During batting practice one of our players was having a hard time making contact. From the top of the hill came derisive laughter. And, with every missed swing, the voice became louder and more offensive. I told the voice to shut up. It only became louder. When Doris began to cry I lost it, telling the big mouth on the bike to "shut the hell up." "Who's going to make me," shouted the mouth. "I will" said I, "right after practice."

Bullies are usually big guys or they are older than their buddies. They have a built-in edge that carries them. Ronnie Rites from 128 South Loudon Avenue was beyond being a bully. He was just plain tough. If you looked up tough guy in the dictionary, his picture would be there. He was called "The Rock" before we had Marciano and Stallone. And, I had just declared publicly that I would silence him. As he rode away on his bike, I hoped that maybe it would be all over, forgotten, ended. Putting the bats and balls away, I gazed up at the #71 hill. No such luck. There he was, waiting for me, along with his brothers and sisters and, seemingly, every kid in Irvington. There was no way out. I got ready to take an ass whipping. Ronnie came out bare-chested, ready for action. I kept my Cub Scout T-shirt on. A show of bravado was far from my mind. Ronnie was a little bigger and started firing haymakers from all angles as I back-pedaled post haste. But the screams for blood from his crowd got my dander up, plus

156

I didn't cotton to getting pummeled. I began to fight back. Encouragement came from the Megary Midgets but this was clearly Ronnie's home ground. His house was only a few hundred feet from #71. Ronnie was inflicting some pain on my head as the crowd roared and grew to mob-like proportions. Ronnie's sisters Gloria, Charlotte, Lois and Janie were screaming so loud I thought they were going to join the battle. The fight carried on for a long time. There were no clinches, wrestling or scuffling. It was just him, and me avoiding the bombs, then counter-punching as the crowd closed in on us. The fight and the ring of spectators moved all the way around the school.

After about half an hour, two very tired kids slowed down to a crawl, still posturing with fists up but dead on our feet. I pushed Ronnie hard and he fell over the hedges and, as I jumped on him, cooler heads prevailed. "Shugie" Kroger jumped in and said, "enough." We actually shook hands and the crowd, now numbering close to a hundred, dispersed and I remember them applauding. Shugie must have really enjoyed the show as he ordered two snowballs for us from the Gyp Joint down the street. The next day my whole body was sore and my face was swollen. Years later, when discussing that evening with Ronnie's brother Jackie and how I thought the fight was a draw, he looked at me and just laughed.

Many times the residue of conflict becomes respect. Ronnie and I became very good friends and for several years were best friends. Mr. Rites, who was known as "The Chief" tended bar at Goetze's on Route #40 in Ellicott City. On Friday nights he would let Ronnie drive his two-tone blue and white Olds. After all the promises and admonishments to be careful, etc., Ronnie would wheel the Olds out of the parking lot and we would cat around all night, radio blaring, with all the windows down. From the Arbutus Teen Center to the Catonsville Toll House we covered a lot of ground until it was time to pick up "The Chief." Ronnie could dance up a storm – Jitterbug, Boogie, Shag, Waltz and Slow, you name it. Taught by his sisters, Ronnie was a natural on the dance floor. Despite many a night at his house, the sisters could never rearrange my two left feet and lack of rhythm. Ronnie loved to imitate Elvis and, with his wavy-haired pompadour, he had that aura. He was a great Elvis impersonator before the actual cult started. And he could hit a golf ball a country mile.

As he grew up, Ronnie was still aggressive and never took a back seat to a challenge. If anyone came up too close to the Olds at a red light, he would not hesitate to fly out of the car and challenge the driver, regardless of who he might be. Being with Ronnie was always "contest living." One Sunday, during an amateur football game at Slentz Field, he spent the entire game on the sideline razzing several players on the Hampden Rams team. Hampden guys were not to be trifled with. Oblivious, Ronnie ignored the groundswell of people forming around us on the sidelines. When the game ended the entire Hampden team sprinted over to our spot. We were completely surrounded in a very small circle. I felt that old #71 feeling again. But Ronnie would not back down an inch as he tried to dictate the terms as to how we would settle this fracas. Fortunately, a squad car with siren blaring drove right onto the field, saving our hides.

Ronnie's other passion was Poly. Not a great student, he did have a knack for Math. Living in the shadow of Mt. St.

Ronnie Rites, pictured in his Poly football uniform, was tough, brash and, seemingly, always looking for a fight. He went from my foe to my close friend. Eventually, I would become his Godfather when he became a Catholic... Rites Family Collection

Joe, a place not readily available to him, Ronnie did the best thing he could do – he went to Poly where he lettered in golf and football. Poly was a powerhouse team and drew students from all over the city. He made the team as a reserve halfback. In his senior year against champion Patterson, with Tech behind, Coach Bob Lumsden put in Ronnie. He gained over one hundred yards and almost broke one. I will never forget late in the game on a cold, gray afternoon in Memorial Stadium, with the outcome long decided, number 46 for Poly walking over to the Patterson bench and delivering a full-blown diatribe to their entire team and coaching staff. Long before trash talk became fashionable, Ronnie had the knack and the guts.

In his early 20's, Ronnie became a Catholic. He lived in the shadow of the imposing St. Joseph's Monastery Church. He was Baptized in the middle 50's. I was his Godfather (Compare).

Ronnie married twice. His first wife Jackie passed away in 1997. They had two children, Chrissy and Bo, and five grandchildren.

In 2000, he married Brenda Simmons who was with him when he passed away in the winter of 2002. He was 65. He battled cancer with the same passion he displayed in life. He was said to have a big mouth, but his smile and heart were far bigger.

Irvington

"Irvington guys always seemed a little eccentric. Sports minded, fun loving guys who always took a dare or played a practical joke, never ones to choose academics over a good time, or so it seemed."

Riding west up Frederick Avenue on the noisy #8 streetcar you cross Caton Avenue, a half mile above old St. Mary's Industrial School where Babe Ruth once roamed. A block later on the right is Duffy's Tavern, known for great seafood and immortalized by the early TV show of the same name. Surrounded by three large cemeteries and three smaller ones, there are nearly a million grave sites spread out over 600 acres, all within a 10-mile radius. You are approaching God's country, literally.

Tucked into the Southwest corner of Baltimore City, Irvington is an eerie, spiritual place. At one end of Frederick Avenue is the sprawling campus of Mount St. Joseph's High School and, just a short walk away, is a huge tract that composes the St. Joseph Monastery churches and grammar school. One of Baltimore's fragmented neighborhoods, Irvington was as unique and self sufficient as any small American town between the two great wars. Her main drag was not more than a quarter mile long, offering a little of everything. The watering holes were the Kozy Klub, The Loop, named after the streetcar turnaround at her doorstep, and the infamous Half Mile Track Saloon. Near the Half Mile was a bowling alley, a drug store and the beloved Irvington Theater that was so cheap (10¢ in 1945) sneaking in wasn't worth the effort. At night the thoroughfare was bathed in a yellowy glow of neon signage struggling to stay bright beyond its Depression era limits. In mid-block was the Irvington Delicatessen, affectionately known as "The Del," run by Hans Heinz, a Bing Crosby look-a-like. It was our weekend hang-out as teenagers. Coming home from a movie, a game, or a date, everyone stopped in to "The Del."

Across the street was a huge brick street car barn extend-ing back a full city block. The skylight was so high that only the most prodigious stone throw could reach it. Those broken windows reflected the hard scrabble nature of the kids living in this neighborhood. Next to the car barn that

The Irvington Theater served as the centerpiece of downtown Irvington, during the 40's and 50's. This quarter-mile strip was the center of our universe — a place where we found entertainment, as well as interesting characters and adventures while coming of age in West Baltimore.

housed dozens of #8 streetcars was the Alco Lunch, a greasy spoon that stayed open all night and made a living off the trolley conductors and the local drunks. None of us ventured in there late at night. Inebriated citizens would come spilling out of the Kozy Klub and the Half Mile Track. Sometimes neighborhood kids would take advantage of those who couldn't stand on their own two feet. Up the street from "The Del" was a corner grocery store with a sawdust floor and across the street was the Irvington Federal bordered by a hardware store, a High's Ice Cream parlor and a liquor store on the corner of Frederick and Collins Avenues. On the North corner was a large Esso station that always had cold sodas and next to the Irvington was Leidig's Drug Store, a tiny hole in the wall with booths and 10¢ Cherry Cokes. The table tops were carved up with initials and love notes from times past. Across from the Esso was the Irvington Pharmacy, a serious place for prescriptions. Tim Cragg was the pharmacist. For a while they had a soda counter but it became obsolete as the space was needed for health supplies. This was a sure sign, even in the early 50's, that Irvington had an aging population.

The neighborhood was mostly Irish, German and poor white migrant types. There was a sprinkling of Italian families. On a Friday night, with the noise and smell of the "iron horses" being herded into the car barn, young people congregating at the movies, drunks coming out of the dives and with shady characters around the Alco Lunch at all hours, in that eerie florescent glow, Irvington seemed to have a little Dodge City in its veins. At the Del we would swap stories of fun, games, conquests and exaggerations. Guys began to shape their persona, talking about hopes and dreams no matter how far fetched. And for a buck you could eat your fill. If you were near broke you could gain sustenance on Heinz's french fries and gravy for only a quarter with a free ice water chaser.

In high school my life centered around the parish and basketball. I played for our CYO team. We were good, winning the City CYO title and representing Baltimore in the Mid-Atlantics in Philadephia. Our coach was an astute Irish philosopher named Joe Fitzgerald, who stressed the fundamentals and just enough discipline to keep our wild rabble in tow. Mike Sneeringer, Ottie McGee and Billy Baquol were outstanding athletes. We could have beaten most high school teams. In fact, Sneeringer, who was cut by St. Joe, came out of the armed forces bigger and stronger and starred at Loyola College under Lefty Reitz, captaining the team and overshadowing the Mt. St. Joe starting five who all matriculated to Loyola.

In 1952, Father Leo Vanston from Scranton, Pennsylvania enlisted me to coach our eighth grade parish team. It was a challenge I readily accepted. It changed my life. Between playing and coaching I was spending all my time in "The Hall." It was also used for assemblies, movies, variety shows, dances, bull and oyster roasts and a Passion Play during Easter. It was always dusty and smelled of stale beer. But I now had my own keys to the building. Keys to a new world. No longer would I have to sneak through open windows and "shimmied" doors. No longer would Mr. O'Brien, the janitor, chase me out. I was eighteen with my own gym. From that point I was no longer the little Italian kid on Hilton Street. I was a coach.

We practiced every day like a high school or college

Top: *A majestic view of St. Josesph's Monastery as seen gazing down Massachusetts Avenue and a peek at the rear of the infamous trolleycar barn (right). Bottom: The 1954 St. Joseph's Monastery City CYO 16-18 Championship team. From left to right, Coach Joe Fitzgerald, Paul Baker, Jack Finnegan, Bill Airey, Tom O'Brien, Frank Luber, Joe Saverino, Bill Baquol, Art McGee and Mike Sneeringer.*

squad. Emulating the Rocket with all his Track & Field manuals, I read every basketball book I could find for drills, styles and systems of play. I had my own laboratory and school work became secondary. Basketball was a way of life in our parish during those days. Back in the late forties and early fifties our girls' teams were tremendous. They were supported by Father John Francis (he used to light up a victory cigar long before Red Auerbach) and coach Frannie Dixon. Paul Cummings, Timmy Hodge and Bill Regan were on my team and went on to play in high school and college. In a two year span we won 61 games and lost four.

Eventually I went on to coach at Towson Catholic High School, Baltimore University, Wheeling Jesuit University and George Washington University. My whole life revolved around basketball. It was my motivation to get an education

1953-54 Mount St. Joe Parochial League Regular Season & Tournament Champs (23-1); (right to left) John Killen, Jim Blair, Jim Gamber, Rick McDonnell, Bobby Vaeth, Tim Hodge, Jack Lauer, Bill Regan, Joe Vogelsang, Rich Kohlhepp, Coach Paul Baker

and it taught me people skills. Similarly, other Irvington guys sought their niche. Many of them hitched-hiked "out the road" to Catonsville's Rolling Road Country Club to caddy and learn golf. Jackie and Ronnie Rites and their cousin Danny O'Brien, plus Jack Corbitt and his cousin Butch Smith come to mind. Jack became the Maryland Scholastic Association champ from St. Joe and won a golf scholarship to the University of Maryland. Danny and Butch became golf professionals and over the years Jackie won many prestigious area titles. Jackie was a great athlete who never went to high school. Self taught, he could do anything. Shoot a basketball, throw a football, run all day, you name it.

Irvington guys always seemed a little eccentric. Sports minded, fun loving guys who always took a dare or played a practical joke, never ones to choose academics over a good time, or so it seemed. They were always ready to compete or to party. Maybe it was all the spirits roaming around those overpowering "bone yards" that clogged their senses.

Three local Irvington champs
(left to right) All MSA Guard Tom Kohlhepp, 1955; MSA Track Standout Mark O'Hara, 1950; and golf prodigy Jack Corbitt, MSA Champ, 1952

Mount St. Joe Football Players
from Irvington
1945-1970 / World War II to Vietnam

Ends
Joe Bach
Gene Nieberlein
Joe Saverino
Richard Sneeringer

Linemen
Frannie Batz
Lou Becker
Georgie Benkert
Jim Blair
Jack Burbank
Joe Fitzgerald
Vince Corbi Kelly
Al Kipke
John Magrogan
Howard Nichols
Jack Uhler

Quarterbacks
Jerome "Butch" Hannon
Tom Kohlhepp
Whitey Zentgraf
Dan Witt

Halfbacks
Joe Bateman
Paul Baker
Herb Duvall

Fullbacks
Tom Bateman
Kenny Kaminsky

Gene Nieberlein

Joe Saverino

Tom Kohlhepp

Paul Baker

High School Basketball Standouts
from Irvington
1945-1970 / World War II to Vietnam

Paul Cummings

Danny DuVall

Al Becker - St. Joe

Billy Baquol - Calvert Hall

Paul Cummings - St. Joe

Don Corbitt - Loyola

Jack Corbitt - Calvert Hall

Frank Dickson - St. Joe

Danny DuVall - Towson Catholic

Herb DuVall - St. Joe

John Ford - Calvert Hall

Jerome "Butch" Hannon - St. Joe

Tim Hodge - Calvert Hall

Gary Hurley - Edison Vo-Tech

Tom Kohlhepp - St. Joe

Art McGee - Poly

Al Neville - St. Joe

Gene Nieberlein - St. Joe

Bill Regan - Loyola

Bill Sass - Calvert Hall

Richard Sneeringer - St. Joe

George Vaeth - St. Joe

Buck Ward - St. Joe

Dan Weber - St. Joe

Danny Witt - St. Joe

Tim Hodge

Bill Sass

Butch Hannon, former St. Joe quarterback and hoop guard, as the leader of the famous Irvington Clowns, circa 1957.

George Young, the former Calvert Hall and City College coaching icon who went on to Hall of Fame status as General Manager of the New York Football Giants, always said that "Irvington guys" were a breed apart from all other kids from Baltimore's city of neighborhoods. In his description he used the word eccentric. In the late 50's Jerome "Butch" Hannon founded "The Irvington Clowns" basketball team. Clad in pajamas and other crazy costumes, they toured the City and surrounding counties with a Globe Trotter style that drew large crowds.

Of all the guys who played in "The Hall" Tom Kohlhepp was the cheese. He was a grade behind in school and a step ahead on the court. Countless hours of practice made him a Basketball Jones before they coined the term. He played on the St. Joe varsity for four years and is a member of the school's Athletic Hall of Fame. He could have played at a higher level. As TV clouded our senses, the memory of Tom's quick release two-hand set shot and needle-threading passes still remain fresh in my memory bank.

I spent a lot of time in the New Cathedral Cemetery, a place where Louis and Adelina Lolli, both my parents and uncles Nick and Arnold are resting. There is a section of Italian graves – people who came over in the last wave of immigration, in the late 19th and early 20th centuries. Their stones are ornate. Marble statues of saints and angels guard the tombs and portraits of the deceased are often inserted in the stones. Always emotional and ritualistic, the Italians stand out even in a potters field of thousands upon thousands.

The caretaker of New Cathedral was Leo Bateman, a tough, crusty old timer whom we affectionately called, "The Beetle." In an old frame house on the cemetery grounds he raised thirteen children. I went to grammar school with Eddie and Anne and became close friends with Joe and his kid brother Tommy. I ate many a meal at Agnes Bateman's "boarding house" table where the food was plain, but plentiful, and delicious. Her style and approach mirrored the way big families of modest means sustained themselves in our country. I was always made to feel welcome, so prying open those huge iron gates on Old Frederick Road was worth it. Right over the cemetery fence were the Uplands Community outdoor courts where we gathered almost nightly in the spring and summer to play some hellacious basketball games. On the hill above the courts was the brand new state-of-the-art Edmondson High School, where Tommy Bateman would become their first legitimate star in football, basketball and lacrosse. When night fell on the courts we went down Woodington Road to the Loop, a neighborhood bar in the basement of a corner house on Frederick Avenue, directly across from St. Joe. The side entrance on Woodington opened its doors to all of Irvington's "grown kids" and a following of nurses, classmates and extended family groups. From around 1950 to 1970 it was the place to be in West Baltimore. Ginny Flannery, a sweet lady who inherited the place when her husband passed away, ran the raucous bar with style and grace and always managed to keep the rabble in order, at least on most nights. She reminded me of Miss Kitty on Gunsmoke. Anyway, the kids who used to roll the drunks at the Kozy and the Half Mile now had their own watering hole, but as we all know, nothing lasts forever.

There is no longer an Irvington of our youth. The car barn gave way to a food market. Heinz died, the watering holes dried up and the Irvington Theater has become The Grace of God International Church of Christ. The Monastery church, which filled to capacity on most Sundays, plays to a skimpy audience and St. Joe is now bordered by fences.

The Bateman's, circa 1944 – My second family... one of the largest of the typical Irvington Irish/German families.
Row 1 (l to r) Eddie, Joe, Agnes, Ann, Donald, Tommy
Row 2 (l to r) Leo, Dick, Paul, Mary, Leo Sr., Agnes (holding Ben), Jack, Patti

Many Irvington guys are living in exile in Catonsville and Howard County. But, everyone has their memories, memories of growing up in an America of plain and easy decisions.

A vestige of tradition still remains on Augusta Avenue, a beautiful, 40-foot wide boulevard with stately trees on both sides. The Victorian homes are set back from the street giving a relaxed look of days past as it slants gently down to Frederick Avenue for about a quarter mile. From its upper end, on a clear day, you can see the Baltimore skyline and harbor. Perhaps this explains why the captains of clipper ships of the late nineteenth century bought homes in Irvington, traveling up Pratt Street from the harbor to Frederick Avenue. God's country. Norman Rockwell would have agreed.

People & Places of Irvington

On the corner... and near corners where things happened.

Maranto's: Old Frederick Road and Morley Streets across from St. Joseph's Monastery School... A Mom & Pop store run by Mom and Pop Maranto and their teenage son Robert. This shop was a precursor to the modern day 7-11. Leo (Pop) Maranto was a commanding presence. Dispensing sandwiches, sundries and free advice, he was a tall imposing man with a white apron and a ready smile, putting his own Italian spin on the events of the day. To me he was a cross between Milton Berle and Jackie Gleason. Maranto's was the Saturday morning port of debarkation for trips and games. Pop showed no favoritism. He blistered everyone in a good natured cacophony of satire. (Above, Pop Maranto is pictured with his oldest son, Leo, who was a Drum Major with the St. Joseph's Monastery Drum Corps.)

Bud's: Just up the street on Old Frederick Road and Monastery

Avenue... This was a confectionery store directly across from St. Joseph Monastery Church, owned and operated by Bud Crocken, his wife and two daughters. It was a place we met on weekend nights to go to movies, games and parties. And, on Sundays before and after Mass, it was the perfect spot to observe the passing parade into church. There was even a ledge where we could sit – our own church pew, so to speak. Many a time our pastor, Fr. Adrion would glare and simmer at the crowd of "no goods" noisily gathering across from his church, at which point we would quickly tramp into Bud's then return when he had left. One night John Ford slipped a 78 record entitled "The Big Brass Band from Brazil" into the pile of Christmas Carols that played from the church loud speakers. I'm sure Fr. Adrion loved that one. Bud was one of the guys. He played softball with us and always had a sympathetic ear to our problems. He even lent guys when they were short.

The Gyp Joint: One half block up from the church on Old Frederick Road... Popular in the mid-40's, this was a tiny hole in the wall across from P.S. #71, just out of range of the church doors. They had pinball machines that paid off, penny candy and cold sodas. It was a hangout for anyone who wanted to skip Mass on Sunday and spend their Collection money. No one ever bragged about going to the Gyp Joint, but everyone had been there. I always felt like I was "going to hell" when I was in the Gyp Joint instead of church.

RU-DOT's Bakery: A half block up from the Gyp Joint on the corner of Loudon Avenue and Old Frederick Road... This was a tiny bakery that sold hundreds of honeydips right out of the oven every day of the week. You could smell the warm sugar from blocks away. Run by Herb van der Berg, whose parents were German immigrants. His kid brother, Otts, was an outstanding golfer and choir singer. The honeydips were 10¢ apiece and three for a quarter. They truly melted in your mouth and it took only two minutes to eat your 25¢ worth.

Doc Kelly's Pharmacy: A tiny drug store on Old Frederick Road across from the Monastery's Grove entrance... Dark and small with a low ceiling, it looked like a 1920's speakeasy. The clanging bell sounded your entry. Doc Kelly would appear behind the soda fountain, silent and seemingly comatose. We would order a phosphate with a mixture of either vanilla, cherry or chocolate flavoring mixed in for only a dime. They had a few booths and I went in several times a week with Hooper, the paper boy, usually at dusk. We would sip the phosphates and talk about football. I never remembered seeing anyone else come in when we were there. Doc Kelly's was spooky to a 12-year old.

Doc Eckhardt's Drug Store: On the corner of Frederick Avenue and Marydell Road... This was where all the St. Joe "boarders" hung out, drinking milkshakes and playing the pinball machines. These were things they didn't have in their native South America.

Coach Tom Armstrong - 8th Grade Coach: was a basketball junkie long before the term was coined. Three nights a week he worked us out in the St. Joe gym. He stressed fundamentals and order, and took no crap from anyone. Subject to mood swings, he could have had a little Bobby Knight in him. Suddenly, at practice, he would stop the action to lecture us about his own "illustrious" past as a great player for Gettysburg College, circa 1921. Then he would resume with vigor. All in all, he was a good coach because he conveyed his passion to us. It is no coincidence that two of his players, Gene Nieberlein and I, went into coaching. Tom Armstrong was always at high school games, arms crossed, chewing his stogie, and wearing that old Art Carney bee-bop hat.

Katie: The DiMario family lived on Mt. Olive Lane, a small side street next to an old cemetery in Southwest Baltimore. Ursalina DiMario and Adelina Lolli spoke the same dialect and shared the same roots. So, it came to pass that Mary Lolli and Katie DiMario would grow up together as close friends. Katie was a tiny, pretty and feisty Italian girl – the kind that always rolled her sleeves up and got into the thick of things. As children, she and Mary were inseparable and the bond always remained. Katie had three kids, Salvatore (Sonny), Eleanor and Francine. Her husband Sam worked in the grocery business in produce and, no matter what the circumstance, he always had a smile. Katie had a big brother who was an amateur boxer and YMCA groupie long before people went to gyms. Lou was always shadow boxing and jogging, getting ready for the "big bout."

Back in the 40's I had a baseball autographed by all the 1944 Orioles, a Triple A team, that was the precursor to the Major League Orioles. They won the "Little World Series" in front of 52,000 people in Baltimore Stadium. One day I came home from school to find Eleanor, Katie's tomboy daughter throwing my prized baseball against the porch steps like it was a tennis ball. On the porch, Mom and Katie were chattering away oblivious to the sacrilege being committed before their eyes. I was furious, smoke coming out of my ears with an urge to choke the life out of Eleanor right there on the spot. The ball was scraped up and the autographs unrecognizable. Holding the damaged sphere in my hands, I learned some valuable lessons that day. "You can't undo what has been done and when you deal with people who do not share your same passion, hold them unaccountable." Also, hide your valuable possessions.

George Kroeger and Tom Lynch, known as Shugies and TL, inherited our 1948 St. Joseph Monastery football team, from the departing Fr. Canice McQuillen. They proved to be excellent coaches and role models, leading us to the 1948 St. Joe League Championship.

St. Joseph's Monastery Parochial School - 1948 St. Joe League Champs.

Row 1 (l to r) Head Coach George "Shugie" Kroeger, Robert Marr, Pete Twardowicz, Micky Beukert, Joe Mannion, Billy Baquol, Ralph Lightner, Larry Holden, Eddie Ball, Assistant Coach Tom Lynch. Row 2 (l to r) Gene Nieberlein, Patty Hannon, Jack Corbitt, Bill Thompson, Charles Riggs, Paul Baker, Tom Kohlhepp, Charles McCurley, Joe Saverino. Missing: Mike Clark, Francis Lightner, Bernie Hodges.

St. Joseph's Monastery Baseball Team - Spring 1947

Row 1 (l to r) George Allulis, Ed Kelly, Bill Boquol, Otts van der Berg, Gene Nieberlein, Bobby Walterhoffer, Paul Baker, Benny Winike, Dave City

Row 2 (l to r) Head Coach Frank Russo, Jimmy O'Hara, George Vaeth, Gene Stallings, Herbie DuVall, Mark O'Hara, Paul Letrise, Jack Burbank, Jim Snyder

The Mount

"In my time, there were students at St. Joe who actually worked a 4:00-12:00 shift in factories and mills."

From the end of World War II to the Korean Crisis, Mt. St. Joseph's High School, in a far off hamlet called Irvington, vibrated with Old World ethnicity. The Xaverian Brothers, who ran orphanages and mill town schools throughout the Eastern United States, were a hardy lot. The spirit of this Order and their modus operandi was based on law and order. Unlike the Jesuits at Loyola High School, who thrived on scholarship and selectivity, and the Christian Brothers of Calvert Hall, who stressed The Golden Rule, the Xaverians were medieval pragmatists. In other words they kicked ass, often.

Blessed with a beautiful campus and a large corps of Brothers (52 by actual count), in their heyday the school attracted hundreds of boys from every parish in the greater Baltimore area. Plus there was a small but feisty crew of boarding students who we derisively named, "The Boarders."

The most significant factor in the school's growth was the #8 streetcar line. Starting in Towson and gerrymandering it's way through the entire city, I called it the Purple and Cream Express. Young freshmen and sophomores without driver's licenses and the poor kids who didn't have wheels made their

177

way to the Mount on the #8. On the school parking lot, it was not uncommon to see five and six students piling out of one car. They came in waves, much like the days of immigration. St. Joe was Ellis Island to the sons and grandsons of our original immigrants, so it was evident that discipline would be administered and swallowed, along with a few well placed whacks now and then.

The Mount offered four courses of study: Academic, Academic Scientific, Commercial and General Course. During this period she was home to nearly 1,000 students, of whom 12% played on one of her many football teams (115 of 970 in 1950). In addition to the best athletes from 40 odd parochial schools, there were two special coaches in place in the persons of Vic Wojciehovski and John Plevyak. Vic was a football star at Notre Dame with roots from Eastern Europe and the West Virginia coal fields. Smoldering and brooding, he was Marlon Brando's "Kowalski" in *A Streetcar Named*

The Parochial School Basketball League

To mine the athletic talent from the city, the Brothers at Mount St. Joseph conducted a Parochial School Basketball League consisting of over thirty grammar schools. The Mount dominated because of that endeavor. The participating schools were from all over the city.

North	South	East	West
Blessed Sacrament	Good Counsel	Holy Rosary	All Saints
Immaculate Conception	St. Jane Frances	Sacred Heart	Ascension
St. Anthony's	St. Jerome's	St. Bridget	St. Agnes
St. Dominic's	St. Mary Star of the Sea	St. Casimir	St. Ambrose
St. Mary's Govans	St. Rose of Lima	St. Elizabeth	St. Benedict
St. Ursula		St. Katherine's	St. Bernadine's
Saints Phillip & James		St. Leo	St. Edward's
Shrine of the Little Flower		St. Patrick's	St. Joseph's Monastery
		St. Michael's Wolf Street	St. Mark's
		St. Wenceslaus	St. Martin

178

Desire. Rough and unapproachable, everyone respected or feared him and he became the role model for the East Baltimore honkies who piled off the #8. He symbolized the Mount in that era and the Brothers loved him.

Brother Anton
"The picture says it all."

If Vic was the thunder of the school, John Plevyak was the fabric. Tall, stately and a bit aloof, John seldom smiled in the classroom or on the playing field. For over forty years he taught the Business courses of typing and shorthand. He was, by far, the best teacher I ever had. Mr. Chips with a typewriter. In addition to his teaching skills, John racked up dozens of championships in soccer and baseball. His messages were always clear and concise. He showed no favoritism and was short on praise. As a senior baseball player, it was apparent that I was not in his plans as a regular. Knowing that I coached my parish grade school team and had a penchant for it, he took me aside and made me his third base coach, pinch runner and utility man. He elevated my self-image at a time when it was diminishing and taught me how to face responsibility and to think ahead. We won the MSA title and I was able to contribute, thanks to John Plevyak. The way that I interacted with my players during my high school and college coaching career had a lot to do with Plevyak's influence. For over 50 years, John Plevyak was Mount Saint Joe. He passed away in May 2000. The Monastery Church was full.

The Brothers were another trip altogether. Many of them were grumpy and resigned to their lot. They were watchdogs with varying pedigrees. They played favorites and there were those who meted out corporal punishment. A very human bunch.

The Principal, when I enrolled in 1949, was Brother Anton, a dark complected Italian. His other title was Prefect of Discipline. Living in the neighborhood, I knew the Mount grounds like the back of my hand. I had been to the top of the Tower, drank wine out at the tackling dummy and knew every window and door in the place, and the ones that could be easily opened. Often, Tom Kohlhepp and I would sneak into the gym late at night, put on the single spotlight and shoot baskets into the wee hours, several stories below the sleeping Xaverians.

Brother Anton used to referee the grade school football and basketball games so he knew me early on. I figured I had an edge when school started. The first time I was summoned to his office, I was loose and relaxed and actually smiling. When he wrapped his forearm tightly around my neck and lifted me off the floor, whispering in my ear, "Saturday morning at eight," I knew then that he played no favorites. After the first year, Anton left for the African missions. His replacement was Brother Cyril, a tall, gangly guy with no sense of humor and no personality. By the end of my freshman year I had been exposed. Not big enough to be a top athlete and a poor student who was constantly under foot, I was unofficially deemed a pain in the ass by the Xaverians. Most of them had their favorites and favorite groups and I belonged to none of them. So it became a fait accompli that I would be an athletic wannabe and a troublemaker. But, somewhere along the way, I learned from Vic and John. My senior year, I found a mentor, someone who elevated my self-worth. His name was Brother Austin, alias Victor Rahm from Brooklyn, New York. A basketball fanatic, he had watched me coach the St. Joseph's Monastery grade school team to the St. Joe Parochial League title. We talked basketball. He gave me books, took us to games, and told me that I had potential. His encouragement pushed me to college. He actually came to dinner at our house. Very few Americani set foot in our house, much less as a dinner guest. But, because he was clergy, at my urging, Adelina acquiesced. My education came from my father and from reading. The Xaverian Brothers could not get through to me in the classroom. You could say I was self- educated Sicilian style, "testa duro" (hard head).

The school cafeteria was a cramped underground cellar with a low ceiling. Invariably, the Americani kids would get into the cafeteria line for their lunch. The ethnic East Baltimore types had the full lunch pails or paper bags bulging with Old World delights. Some of the bags would be soaked through from the olive oil and garlic. The smells would hit the ceiling then come back down to ground zero. The pungent aroma reminded one of an Italian deli, the kind Adelina used to drag me through when I was a kid. By the middle of the week the cafeteria smelled like the hold of a trans-Atlantic freighter. Add in carbonated drinks and these kids would become walking gas bombs by the fifth period. If guys weren't "blowing off steam," they were nodding off. Then some of the more sadistic Brothers would remove the gloves and take target practice on sleeping heads. The final bell at 2:40 was always a relief as everyone scattered for home,

Mount St. Joe All-Italian Football Team

E	T	G	C	G	T	E
Joe Saverino 1952-54	Bill Lombardi 1949-52	Harry Ilardo 1971-72	Ben Petrilli 1950-53	Mike Tirocchi 1959-61	Vince Trombetta 1948-49	Noel Sabatino 1960-63

QB
Frank Tamburello
1948-51

HB
John Geppi
1945-47

HB
Vince Merlo
1956-57

FB
Vince Rosetti
1946-48

Honorable Mention:

Frank Geppi
1948-49

Frank Lancelotta - G
1955-56

Izzy Trovato
1939-42

Among the ethnics were some excellent Italian athletes. These guys came from all over the City to play for the Mount.

*Not responsible for Italians with Anglo names and my loss of memory.

182

work, or the playing fields. In my time there were students at St. Joe who actually worked a 4:00 to 12:00 shift in factories and mills.

In 1949, one of my closest friends, Gene Nieberlein, from our parish came

(left to right) Br. Ricardus, John Plevyak and Vic Wojciehovski celebrate more gridiron and soccer success for the Gaels.

to St. Joe. From a poor family situation, he was on an athletic scholarship. A tall German kid with wide shoulders and a cold stare, Gene became a star. He was the favorite of Vic and the St. Joe Brothers. St. Joe was his second home. All through high school, Gene worked an outside job of some sort. He grew up quick. After college he succeeded Vic as Head Basketball Coach and, eventually, Athletic Director and Football Coach. He was at St. Joe as a student, coach, AD and parent for over 40 years. He won his share of titles, but more important he kept discipline at a school that was losing it, along with the attrition of the religious presence. Gene and his wife, Pat Swiston, raised seven children. All of his sons were outstanding student athletes at the Mount. And Chris and Gene have joined their father in the school's Athletic Hall of Fame.

If the old Mount were to be represented in a Mount Rushmore motif, Vic, John and Gene would be the faces.

Hal Sparks

In 1971, St. Joe hired an "unknown outsider," named Hal Sparks. For the next decade he personally elevated the St. Joe athletic program to high water marks not seen since the 1940's and 50's.

On the sheer power of positive energy, he coached football (67%), wrestling (90%), baseball (86%) and track (88%) to unprecedented heights. In addition, he was a great fundraiser and went the last mile to get his players into college. "Probably more important than Hal's won-loss record as a coach was the way he cared about his players in hope of getting athletic scholarships for as many players as possible," stated Dave Etheridge.

His efforts pushed St. Joe into modern times, helping her continue as a viable institution.

The fourth one would undoubtedly be Brother Ricardus, a spindly little fireball with the metabolism of a humming bird. He taught Latin to the college bound students and was omnipresent as the Athletic Director. No one wanted to win more than Ricardus. He paced the sidelines, sleeves rolled up, spitting nails and hurling invectives. He and Vic were two of a kind. Up until I made the football team Ricardus didn't know who I was. After that, I got an occasional nod. I could always gauge how I stood with "Kowalski" by the way Brother Ricardus said hello to me.

The St. Joe gym was something out of the Roaring 20's. In fact, it looked like the garage where Al Capone ordered the St. Valentine's Day Massacre. The court was about 84 feet long by 44 feet wide, but the close proximity of the walls made the playing area even smaller. Truly a bandbox, the Mount seldom lost on it's home floor. Wedged into the side of a hill, it seemed to buttress the entire school complex, which leaned down hard on its north wall. The gym consisted of one regulation size basketball court, a few offices, a music room, an equipment room, and locker rooms. There were stands behind one basket where 100 people could sit. At the other end sat the two team benches and score keeper's table. Both sidelines were framed by brick walls, just a foot or two from the out of bounds line. On the north wall was a concrete trough to catch the residue from the sweating bricks. Above the team benches was a balcony with four rows of seats. The balcony was connected to the courtyard, which leaned down onto the gym. The courtyard was framed in a wooden canopy. It looked like a small prison yard or a medieval stable. Above it all was the symbolic Mount Tower, which still stands today. In 1950, this place wreaked of the 20's. The courtyard was the true melting pot of the Mount. Guys would congregate there before school, just hanging out, copying homework, drinking coffee , smoking cigarettes, girding up for the combat at hand with the Xaverians. Pedigreed Catonsville "richies" bonded with East Baltimore "greasers," many of whom were wearing family hand-me-downs. The courtyard was where pep rallies and lunch periods were held. Babe Ruth played on the Mount baseball field in 1915 and was said to have been seen "hanging out" in that very court-yard. And below, in the antiquated torture chamber of a gym, some stirring events took place. None more memorable than the Southern High versus Mt. St. Joe wrestling match on February 10, 1949. In the 165 pound class Southern featured Ernie Fisher, a truly great undefeated wrestler who would later star at the University of Maryland and compete in the 1956 Olympics in Australia. Ernie was a rangy, angular band of solid muscle and, with his wavy blond pompadour, looked just like Lex Barker, the guy who succeeded Johnny

185

Weismuller as Tarzan. He sure didn't look like a high school student.

His opponent that day was Jack Shanahan, the Mount's football captain and All-MSA pulling guard. He sported thick muscles and a perfect flat-top any Marine would kill for. Ernie was a stud but Jack was right there with him. The match had some good bouts, as our Vince Kelly from Irvington beat Fisher's brother Bobby that day on his way to a career where he narrowly missed the Olympic team in 1956. But on this day, everyone was there to see Fisher and Shanahan. It was about 4:30 on a chilling February afternoon, with the Winter Solstice closing in on the upper windows. The steaming radiators hooked up high on the south wall seemed to emit eerie noises, as if in their own inanimate way, they too craved the impending action. I was a thirteen year old eighth grader seated not more than twenty feet from the mat, sitting

In 1949, Mount St. Joe's Jack Shanahan (left) and Southern's Ernie Fisher (right) met in a legendary encounter in the St. Joe gym. Despite the support of a frantic crowd from Shanahan's corner, Fisher scored a 5-3 decision. Later the two became teammates at the University of Maryland.

on my book bag. People were shoehorned into the gym, hanging from every nook and cranny. Norman Rockwell would have had a field day. The crowd was abuzz with tension. When Shanahan drove Fisher off the mat with a vicious leg tackle, Ernie's pompadour shook loose

along with the pent-up emotions of the roaring students. And when they both hit the mat, the ceiling lights flickered. I began to worry about the building collapsing. With every move and counter move, the students would roar. A wave of noise would erupt and subside over and over. The Brothers were leaning out the music room windows on the South wall, screaming their lungs out. People were truly hanging from the rafters. With no room for the noise to escape, it continued to reverberate off the walls like an out of control roller coaster. Shanahan and Fisher were locked in a life and death struggle, neither giving an inch. In the second period Shanahan nearly pinned Fisher and the noise reached a crescendo. As time wound down, Shanahan barely missed an escape move that would have tied the match. Fisher escaped with a narrow 5-3 victory and was mobbed by his teammates. His fancy hairdo in complete disarray, and his faced flushed, he hardly looked like the winner. Shanahan walked impassively off the mat to the ringing sounds of approval from the Mount faithful. Years later I learned that Jack Shanahan's father came to see the match. It was the first time he had ever seen his son wrestle or play any sport for that matter. In the post Depression era there was no time for people to be Little League Parents. Food had to be put on the table. Also in retrospect Jack Shanahan recalled going to a semi-pro football dinner many decades later where a group of Southern High alums recalled the match with great relish and seemingly remembered every detail. It was an event for the ages with no admission.

Before characterizing the Mount as a jock school, one must look a little deeper. As Bear Bryant once said, "No one ever rallied around a math class." And the Mount and her graduates throughout the years have certainly rallied around her athletic teams. Sports and it's headlines drew a steady stream of students. The school flourished and education was present and accounted for. To say that athletics has made St. Joe the school that it is today would not be too far from the truth.

"We're from the Mount and we couldn't be prouder," so the chant goes. But education is the sum total of all one's experiences and the Mount gave us all experiences that will last a lifetime.

The Magazines

"Life Magazine was graphic, emotional, photo journalism. In its time it was USA Today and CNN rolled into one."

Born in 1935, I grew up with *Life Magazine. Life's* first issue was November 23, 1936. In his thirst for knowledge, my father religiously read the newspapers and kept the house filled with periodicals. He subscribed to *Life* immediately, and every week, like clockwork, this pictorial history of what was happening in America, and around the world, was placed on our doorstep. *Life Magazine* was my Dad's educational vehicle and my storybook.

In addition to soaking up all the info, Dad was a collector. There were 52 issues per year and every year he would wrap up each year's volumes in brown paper, tie them with kite cord, label the year, and push them up into the garage loft. Eventually, they began to take on a life of their own. Heaven forbid if we lost track of a *Life* magazine. They were always referred to as "the magazines." Grandma Lolli irreverently gave them a wide berth, along with an "Italian salute." But they endured, every last one of them.

Life Magazine was graphic, emotional, photo journalism. In its time it was USA Today and CNN rolled into one. It provided a young child with a window to the world. It was also one of the few ways in which I bonded with my father.

When we moved in 1956, "the magazines" were taken down from the loft with care. Our new modern duplex did not have a garage. The loft had kept the magazines dry and Dad's packing kept them flat and clean. Now the collection had to be placed in the basement of our new home, exposed to dampness and mildew. Twenty years of *Life,* from 1936 to 1956, amounted to over 1,000 magazines – 1,040 to be exact.

By 1971 the collection began to overrun the basement. The number reached 1,820. My father was now 62 years old. *Life Magazine* was losing its popularity. I was moving my family to a new job in West Virginia. Taking the collection with me was out of the question. We decided on a sane, educational choice. We would give the entire collection to my current employer, the University of Baltimore.

With the opening of the new Langsdale Library, it seemed like a welcome addition. Mr. Nicholson, the Head Librarian, accepted the gift. It seemed the right thing to do. Shortly after, my father received a short thank you acknowledgment letter. It seemed such a small gesture for such a big gift. It represented the fabric of our lives, the symbol of our evolution, our bonding clay. I felt empty, but moved on to reality in West Virginia. I forgot the trauma of "letting go," but whenever I would see Life, my psyche kept tweaking. *Life* stopped its long run in 1972, 1,864 copies, and P.B. Sr. had every one.

Early in the 1980's, upon returning from West Virginia, I realized that my parents' basement had more room. I wondered about Baltimore University and the collection. One Sunday I attended a Baseball Card Flea Market in Pikesville. I was drawn toward a stand that displayed *Life* magazines.

As I perused the issues, I was shocked to see my father's subscription stickers on the right-hand corners of these issues. Baltimore University had microfilmed them and sold off the collection, piece-meal, to collectors. To say the least, it was a sad day.

For the past 15 years or so I have second-guessed myself about the way we released "the magazines." Although they are valuable, there is no real monetary coup there. In retrospect, I would have found a way to preserve them, all 1,864 of them. Since then, I take to buying selected issues at the antique shows my wife drags me to. I have lots of famous sports covers, Blanchard and Davis, plus Johnny Lujack in color, among others. My father passed away in 1995. I never told him. And now, every time I pick up "the magazine" at those musty old stands, looking for our address label, I think of how they shaped our lives.

Billy the Kid

"One night at the Cross Street Pool Hall, on top of a corner grocery store, he was playing an older guy with tattoos a nine ball match for big money."

It's 1953 and the beginning of another steamy Baltimore summer. The air coming through the open ballroom doors offers some relief to the prom couples entwined on the dance floor. On the patio stands Billy Ackiss, puffing a cigarette and staring into the starry night. "Blue Moon" fills the air. Obviously a rebel, he is miles away. He does not mix and does not speak as he stays perfunctorily on the periphery doing his duty, taking the beloved star-crossed love of his life to her senior prom. The kids at this soiree are middle to upper class private school types, all with hopes, dreams, and pedigrees. Tonight they show their youthful, precocious behavior. Billy keeps his distance. James Dean before there was one.

Born and raised on the narrow streets of South Baltimore, a shot and a beer on the waterfront neighborhood, he grew up fast and hard. At night, he shot a mean game of nine ball and during the day Billy inhabited the Cross Street Hall to shoot baskets. When he turned 15, the race track took over. You get the picture.

Saying little, he had a great sense of timing. He spoke with benevolent knowing eyes and when he smiled he warmed the room. Slim of build, he possessed large strong hands and thin wrists. His life early on consisted of clicking cue balls and the staccato dribble of the basketball. He mastered both.

Playing for Southern High School on Friday night public school double headers at Eastern High School, he attracted standing room only crowds. Leaving the nine ball pigeons to ply his other trade, he dribbled the ball with either hand at blinding speed. The sound overpowered the sight. In motion, he passed the ball with heretofore unseen precision. Behind the back, between the legs, you name it, and it was only 1951. Was he out of a space capsule? He was always quiet, calm, and under control on and off the court, so far ahead of his time it was scary.

Billy Ackiss

We were from West Baltimore, me, Jack and Big J, a slight social cut above his upbringing. We knew all the prom queens, yet we hit the streets hard too. To Ackiss we were his bridge, his comfort zone from reality. One night, at the Cross Street Pool Hall, on top of a corner grocery store, he was playing an older guy with tattoos a nine ball match for big money. There was well over $100 on the bar. It seemed like a thousand. Wall to wall people, thick smoke, and only the sound of the clicking ivories.

He banked the nine and swept up the cash. The tension eased, he smiled that little Alan Ladd curl, motioned to the door, and we partied into the night.

Billy never went to college. He went from high school straight to the race track, never stopping to marry the prom sweetheart. Here was a guy whom everyone loved, who never got comfortable with himself. A cold fish with a heart of gold, he ended up in Alaska working some nefarious scams. He used to call a buddy named Lefty to get East Coast results before they hit the ticker tape up there.

Some years later, it was reported that he died in a fire, trying to rescue his son, so they say. Everybody loved Billy.

Hell's Half Acre

"On Saturday nights after the last race at Pimlico, buses would deposit the winners and losers onto East Baltimore Street for a night of pleasures where everyone could be a winner."

Just a few short blocks from Jones Falls, on East Baltimore Street, is the dividing line to Little Italy. Here, according to legend, "Divine Intervention" by St. Anthony saved the Italian immigrants and their homes during the Great Fire of 1904. Less than the length of a football field, this thin strip of carnal debauchery called, "The Block," at one time was the most infamous piece of real estate on the East Coast. Heralded in books, magazines and song, it was our calling card, eclipsing both the Colts and Orioles as Baltimore's number one tourist attraction. Unfortunately, it defined us to the outside world. Baltimore and "The Block" were synonymous. For decades, seamen from hundreds of docking ships, conventioneers and tourists, plus the usual low-life's, combined to make "The Block" unforgettable. Every guy born and raised in Baltimore during the 40's and 50's, at one time or another, made it down to "The Block."

On the front end of the strip, the singular most famous attraction was the Gayety Theater. Her lights shone larger and brighter. On the East Coast circuit it featured a soup-to-nuts burlesque review replete with the bawdy emcee, raunchy comedy scenes and, of course, the professional strippers accompanied by a live orchestra. One could never forget Irma the Body , Tempest Storm, Princess Domay and Pat Holliday.

Between classes, at lunch time and after school, many of the Christian Brothers' finest, the Calvert Hall student body,

Blaze Starr... stopping 'em in their tracks.

would find their way down to the "Block" for some afternoon delight. It was only a ten minute canter from Cathedral and Mulberry streets. All they needed for a free pass back to the classroom from Brother Regis (The Little King) was to be carrying a rosary. So whenever the young Cardinals schlepped off for a quickie at the Gayety, they always remembered to carry a rosary. Debauchery, confession and redemption in the same afternoon. What a life lesson.

The Baltimore Street "Block" was the symbolic icon for sin. All the worldly pleasures could be found inside the inviting doors of the 2 O'Clock Club, The Club Troc, or Murray's Show Bar, so it seemed to a 16-year-old kid from an ethnic, religious family. As I approached "The Block" from the west on a spring night, the bright honky-tonk lights made the area look like a carnival midway. On Saturday nights after the last race at Pimlico, buses would deposit the winners and losers onto East Baltimore Street for a night of pleasures where "everyone could be a winner." It was Hell On Wheels and Sodom and Gomorah rolled up into a neat package of lust and booze.

Walking amidst a wall of people all the cliches "jumped into your face": The guy with ten wrist watches on his arm; the street walker in high heels, mesh nylons and the "butterfly" eyes; the gum-chewing, oblivious cop flipping his billy club; and, of course, the cigar-chomping carny barker urging you into his den of sin. "The Block" placed you smack in the middle of another world.

What if someone saw me? I walked in deeper and deeper and, as the hurdy gurdy music wrapped itself around me, I threw down two bucks and stepped into the 2 O'Clock Club. Inside it was pitch dark like the funhouse at Carlins

Park. It took a few minutes to adjust and focus. The spotlight came on revealing a circular bar and a crowd of shadowy faces. The emcee, on a microphone too loud for the room, introduced "Maria from Korea," who danced across the bar, taking it all off to the tune of "My Blue Heaven." Ordering a beer, I drank it half down in one swig. My hormones hadn't kicked in yet with all that guilt and secrecy stuff to get over. As each act got a little better I tried to relax and ordered a second beer.

By now the hazy smoke and stale air enveloped the room as Blaze Starr appeared from behind a curtain. A short package of red-haired dynamite with great "headlights," she had special gifts and special ways of showing them. She responded to the horny cat-calls with curt one-liners, all the while tantalizing the coarse rabble, never missing her cues. The combination of smoke, stale air, and guilt began to make me dizzy. I needed another cold one but I was broke. Bolting out into the darkness, I took a deep breath of cool air and felt the sweat drying on my brow. I wasn't ready for this. Walking hard up Baltimore Street, looking back at the fading lights and the din of the rabble, I broke into a run, making tracks from Sodom and Gomorrah.

Section IV

"Gente Grande"

Grand Gentlemen

The Linchpin

"Over the years they remained friends, never out of touch... Paulie was always there for him."

Webster describes "linchpin" as a pin inserted in an axle outside of the wheel to prevent the wheel from slipping off the track. For well over a quarter century, Thomas D'Alesandro was the linchpin for Little Italy and the Italian way of life. He lived his entire life at 245 Albermarle Street in the heart of Baltimore's Little Italy, among friends, neighbors and relatives. Throughout his mercurial career, which had him rubbing shoulders and pressing flesh with dignitaries, celebrities, governors and presidents, D'Alesandro never ignored his constituents, his paisanos. He knew only too well how difficult respect and upward mobility was to come by for the Italians of his time. He would not, could not, and did not abandon them. Always accessible, he was a man of the people. Acquiring jobs, raising money, advising and counseling, were always a part of his daily duties. The Italians responded in kind, never doing anything to discredit their "padrone." His dignity and class motivated his constituents to become better people. This dynamic totally overshadowed his huge list of accomplishments during his years in Congress and at City Hall. Giving people a role model and a sense of pride was clearly number one and his most lasting legacy.

The perfect example of Tommy's commitment to St. Leo's was his devotion to the parish school. For over forty years he personally kept the school from closing by raising the money for its upkeep. As long as there were children in the neighborhood, they would have access to a Catholic education.

In 1947, when he was elected Mayor of Baltimore, Little Italy celebrated the event in grand style. Wall-to-wall revelers gathered in the streets and partied into the wee hours. People were hanging out the windows of every row house, waving American and Italian flags. And the Little Italy Drum and Bugle Corps marched the streets all night long. A wave of emotion engulfed the area. One of their own had made it. One who knew them by name and by deed. Truly a night to remember.

In the years before being elected Mayor, Tommy was elected to the U.S. Congress. Living in Baltimore with a growing fami-

With his wife Nancy looking on proudly, Tommy confers with President John F. Kennedy during his days as Mayor of Baltimore.

204

ly, he elected to commute to D.C. from Baltimore's Penn Station. And there, waiting to help him and to "return favors of the past" was one of his paisanos, Paulie Mugavero, alias Paul Baker. They had been boyhood friends. Tommy was five years older and leader of a crew of Italian kids who roamed Lombard Street as "Sabbath Goy," performing Sabbath duties for the many Orthodox Jewish families. They would light the cooking fires, click on the electricity, and perform chores for a few small coins. Over the years they remained friends, never out of touch. Paulie was a Ticket Clerk at the Pennsylvania Railroad Station on Charles Street, a position he held for over 40 years. He organized Tommy's travel plans and schedule. There were times when Tommy had to travel early and return late, or a late session necessitated a travel change. Paulie was always there for him. And there were days when a troubled Tommy would ponder issues and problems that were facing him and needed a sympathetic ear or a sounding board. On those days, Paulie would ride over to D.C. with him, providing the support he needed. My father always spoke of Tommy D'Alesandro with respect and reverence. And I am sure that the aforementioned scenario has been repeated about Tommy and hundreds and maybe thousands of people who had the same experience.

A few winters ago, Tommy's son and also ex-Mayor of Baltimore, attended my annual Basketball Dinner in Little Italy. And last summer we played golf together. Trite as it may sound, I know that our fathers would be very happy with that.

The Godfather
Vince Dundee

"He rose above the rabble with two very obvious qualities, quickness and heart."

Because of Mario Puzo's infamous series, the word Godfather takes on a different connotation. But in the parlance of the Catholic Church, the title of Godfather belongs to the person who represents the new born child at the sacrament of Baptism. He speaks the words of the sacrament as the designated Archangel of the helpless child, bridging the gap of time.

My father sure picked a special person to look over me. Vincent Lazzara, known to the boxing world as Vince Dundee, Middleweight Champion of the World, was my "comparé." I was baptized on October 20, 1935 at St. Joseph's Monastery Church on Old Frederick Road. Dad and Vince were close friends from the old days in East Baltimore and Little Italy. They met as teenagers at the Grand Theater on Conkling Street in Highlandtown.

Vince was among the hundreds of Italian males who would climb into the ring during the Roaring Twenties to seek recognition and make their mark. Prior to this era, Irish fighters dominated. Vince's brother Joe won the World Welterweight title on June 3, 1927 in the Polo Grounds in New York City, outpointing highly touted Pete Latzo of

Scranton, Pennsylvania. In the meantime, Vince had compiled a tremendous record as an amateur. He turned pro and followed Joe out to the West Coast, at that time, the mecca of boxing. Only eighteen, he was nervous about the move, but saw an opportunity to make some money. Real jobs were becoming scarce. As Joe's brother the door of opportunity opened for him. Placed on the undercards of big fights, he began to get noticed. Vince was not your typical old time Depression era banger. His punch was lacking and his frame was slender. He rose above the rabble with two very obvious qualities, quickness and heart.

Bobbing and weaving he made bigger, stronger guys miss and look bad. He would slide along the ropes, always keeping his opponent off balance. Quick feet and hand speed made him a formidable counter puncher who put together classic boxing combinations. Vince fought mostly on the road, on his opponent's turf. In California, the Midwest and against the favorite sons in Eastern cities, he was always up against it. In twelve years of professional boxing he averaged a fight a month, an astounding feat. Vince would invariably win over the home crowd. His clever and crafty skills along with his gentlemanly traits were easy to like. As a gentleman, he was compared, in print, to Gene Tunney several times. Vince amassed a record of 112 victories,

Proud Godparents, Vince and Connie Dundee, with Paulie Mugavero Baker, October 20, 1935... Paulie Mugavero Baker collection

18 losses, 7 draws and 2 no contests. He was knocked out only once.

On October 30, 1933, Vince outpointed Lou Brouillard in Lou's hometown of Boston to win the Middleweight title. Right in the middle of the Great Depression, the nation hardly blinked an eye. He went on to successfully defend the title twice before losing to Teddy Yarosz from Pittsburgh. The fight was held in Pittsburgh, as the challenger's backers offered Dundee a $25,000.00 guarantee. In today's market that equated to about a half million dollars. This time, on the road against a real tough boy, Vince lost the title. There was no rematch clause.

In researching and writing about my Godfather, I came across several outstanding oldtimers who had their own opinions on Baltimore area fighters. Vince only fought in Baltimore as an amateur. After 1925 his career seldom took him back home. To my knowledge he never fought a main event in Baltimore. In addition, he was reaching his peak as the worst depression in our history was upon us. As a result, some of the oldtimers have taken a shot at Vince and his place in boxing history. They remember brother Joe winning the title in the Polo Grounds as a hard body puncher the prototype era fighter. The oldtimers point to the truly great Baltimore fighters like Kid Williams, Joe Gans and Harry Jeffra, and rightfully so. Also, they talk of some great club fighters like Len Mahoney, Jack Portney, Pete Galiano and the Finazzo brothers, who were equal to Vince at some point in time.

But, Vince Dundee took his craft to another level. He moved out of Baltimore – a move not too many from this provincial town were ever wont to do. He took a risk. He

The marriage of Vincent Lazzara and Connie Rossi, 1930
(left to right) Lena Lazzara, Vince's sister and the Maid of Honor, the bride, Connie Rossi of Belleville, NJ, Middle Weight World Champion to be, Vincent Lazzaro Dundee and best man, Paulie Mugavero Baker (age 20).

moved "up town" with his game, out of conjecture and into reality. He stepped up. He then hooked up with crafty management and maximized his potential. For a guy with a tenuous make-up to go as far as he did, winning 112 pro fights and the Middleweight Championship of the World was truly remarkable. The world is filled with conjecture and second guessing. The sporting gentry thrives on it. Vince, however, reached out hard for the brass ring and got it. No oldtimers, or anyone else, could refute his record. Case closed.

Teddy Yarosz

Teddy Yarosz, tough son of a Pittsburgh coal miner couldn't box like Vince, but he was hard as steel. He decisioned Vince three times. Vince also lost two close decisions to Jewish Whirlwind Jackie Fields (Finklestein). Those two guys were a little too much for Vince to handle, in slam-bang bouts that all could have gone either way, and account for five of his 18 professional losses.

Yarosz had a short reign as Middleweight Champ, but he fought into the late 30's as a middleweight and light heavy. He fought Billy Conn three times, winning once. He fought some of the nation's best black fighters who were on the way up, beating legend to be Archie Moore, decisioning standouts Lloyd Marshall and Jimmy Bivins and losing a split decision to Ezzard Charles. All in all, Teddy Yarosz was one tough cookie.

Vince Dundee (left) wading in on Teddy Yarosz during their title fight on September 11, 1934 at Forbes Field in Pittsburgh, PA.

Johnny

"He took care of any Italians who came his way, always ready with a job, a loan, a favor or a small kindness."

Back in the eighties I worked for a few years as a liquor salesman. I had free time – time to reflect and to watch my three sons grow up and play ball. Once a week I would work the Northeast corridor and, if the weather was nice, I would park under a tree in Holy Redeemer Cemetery to read the morning paper and eat lunch. One Spring day a gentle breeze blew across the expanse of endless white stones and down in the valley a solitary figure slowly made his way.

Uncle Mugs and Johnny Pica were inseparable boyhood pals. They would eventually go to War together and Mugs was Johnny's Best Man when he married Antoinette Pellegrini. Mugs and Johnny had their own little gang which made sure the neighborhood ran just right, the way it was supposed to, if you know what I mean.

There were five corners in Little Italy, each with their own crowd. Much like a college fraternity, you belonged to one specific corner. A half century later when Johnny Pica passed away, these same guys gathered on their respective corners once again. For a brief moment time stood still. Then as the bells tolled, they made their way in unison to St. Leo's to pay their final respects. A tender but eerie moment

213

This signed photo to his parents, during his military service, reveals the charm of Johnny Pica.

La Campanile Americana

Johnny Pica's Heroism and the huge turnout of young Italian Americans (1.5 million) in World War II flies in the face of detractors who questioned the fighting resolve of Italians. In the Old Country the Italian man's allegiance stretched only as far as the "Campanile," the sound of his village church bells. In America, his new land, the allegiance stretched much further.

proved, somehow, Johnny Pica had touched them all.

Other than a stint in the Army during World War II, where he became a decorated hero earning the Silver and Bronze Star as well as a Purple Heart, Pica never left Little Italy. His family lived at 244 S. Exeter Street. He and Antoinette had two children, Johnny Jr. and Maria. They lived in Govans, but Johnny was always in Little Italy. He worked for Tommy D'Alesandro and ran his own company, Alpine Construction. He took care of any Italians who came his way, always ready with a job, a loan, a favor or a small kindness. Pica was the life of the party and at weddings he was a one man entertainment center. As a child I attended numerous family weddings and the highlight was when Johnny hit the dance floor. Long and lanky, he had all the moves. He could jitterbug with the best of the blacks and his smooth "shag" had all the women

Always the life of the party, Johnny Pica and his lovely wife, Antoinette Pellegrini Pica, pose for a photographer at another happy occasion.

breathless.

When Johnny Pica walked into a room everything changed. A quip, a look, that deep throaty laugh and wide smile. He was what being Italian was all about. Fun, laughter and good fellowship were his trademarks. The first time I ever saw him he was a gangly teenager, loosey goosey and laughing. As he flew up the steps at 913 Fawn Street, two at a time into the Mugavero kitchen, everyone stopped eating and shouted out their greetings. A place was set and even the staid Salvatora smiled and embraced him.

The guy I saw that day in Holy Redeemer was Johnny Pica visiting Antoinette. As he walked up the hill into close view, I buried my head in the *Morning Sunpaper*. That moment belonged to him and him alone. Johnny Pica and the remaining people like him can never be replaced. Five grand children and both his offspring remain. They all live in America as they should. But, Little Italy still exists and as John Jr. states, "My dad still lives here... I hear his voice in the wind and I expect to see him walking around a corner, or sitting at the end of a bar smiling. Somehow he is still among us."

Where Have You Gone, Perry Como

"Perry was about to sing 'Ave Maria.' You could have heard a pin drop."

Ostensibly unlike rowdies Frank Sinatra and Dean Martin, Perry Como could have been sleeping with Diana Ross for all we knew, but on that show, in prime time on national TV, he was the modern day savior of Italian-American culture.

During the commercials, Grandpop Lolli would go for more Dago Red and the kids would fuss and holler. Then the show would reappear and Adelina's sharp admonishment would signal for "silenzia." Donnie and Marie would give a rousing rendition of "Jingle Bell Rock." Aunt Anna noted that all those little kids who gathered around Perry were not professionals, but relatives and grandchildren.

At 9:50 the living room turned completely still. Everyone straightened up. Luigi put out his cigar and placed his glass of vino on the coffee table. Perry was about to sing "Ave Maria." You could have heard a pin drop. By 9:55 everyone was teary-eyed. Perry Como was a pure Italian who appealed to everyone across our nation. A class act, the personification of our beloved Italian culture - a saint in our midst. Como helped raise the Italian persona to an all time high in America. But nothing lasts forever. Families grow and drift apart. And the old people die. In those days we were so proud to be defined by someone like Perry. When the Perry Como Show left the scene, we began to get

"Transfixed by Perry"! Perry Como (far right) was a hero in our household and we always tried to watch his show. (From left, Jeannette, Adelina and me watching the show... Paulie Mugavero Baker collection (left)

another Italian "slice-of-life." One we didn't like too much. Shows like the Untouchables, the Godfather chronicles and the Sopranos have taken the Italian persona and hung it out to dry for the whole world to see. And, as we move into the 21st Century, Italians are still fighting the stereotype. Just as the Perry Como years were so much fluff, the recent personifications are also out of line. It is a shame that Italian-Americans continue to be defined by the commercialization of Mafia movies and the Sinatra mystique. The National Order of the Sons of Italy does provide a strong voice, both political and symbolic, that our heritage is sacred and special, demanding the respect that our forefathers earned. And now in the 21st Century we are all Americans, and on a global scale, citizens of the world.

With no disrespect to Perry Como, I wish to be defined by my family and my own actions, not by the Mafia or Frank Sinatra, or anyone else for that matter. But surely, if Adelina were alive today she would have uttered the words, "Dove Sei Andato, Perry Como?" (Where have you gone, Perry Como?).

The Voice of Italy
Guy Sardella

"Sardella helped Italian immigrants become acclimated to life in the United States..."

On April 5, 1993 the Italian-American community in Baltimore lost a legend when Gaetano "Guy" Sardella passed away at the age of 80.

Guy was known as the "Voice of Italy" for his 30-plus years as a local radio personality who gave voice to Italian traditions through his weekly show, "The Guy Sardella Original Italian Hour." The program originated in 1940 and ran for well into the 70's on AM stations WCBM and, later, WBMD.

Sardella helped Italian immigrants become acclimated to life in the United States and drew attention in 1944 for his service to Italian prisoners of war being held at Fort Meade in Maryland. He helped the POWs feel at home by forming a soccer team and assembling a marching band.

Also during the war, he taught Italian at the Berlitz School of Languages. In the 1960's, he taught Italian at the Peabody Conservatory of Music and at Baltimore City College.

Through his radio program, he raised money for the American Red Cross and American War Bonds. In 1960 he was named Baltimore's Italian-American of the Year and was twice knighted by the Italian Government. He also received

Guy Sardella

the Star of Solidarity from the Republic of Italy.

Guy was born in Baltimore but went to Italy, at the age of seven, and received his education there. He returned to the U.S. in 1937 and settled in Philadelphia where he immediately became involved in numerous Italian-American ethnic organizations. He also was a correspondent for many Italian-American newspapers, including *Il Progresso,* the largest Italian language newspaper in America.

Everyone in my family spoke of Guy Sardella with reverence. He was our conduit to respectability. He did hundreds of little things for hundreds of people. He pointed the way for Italians in the 30's, 40's and 50's. He was particularly helpful for the immigrants who were still coming over at that time. In the Italian community if there was a problem, the first option was Guy Sardella, a soft spoken gentle man. He was from Adelina's home town of Teramo and when he came through our door, we rolled out the red carpet.

Rocky & Benny

"In Trotta, Rocky found a true-blue guy. He was tired of big-timers and phonies."

Right after Grandpop Lolli passed away, television began to replace radio. Instead of "Joe Louie's" Bum of the Month Club, that was sprinkled with such Italian stalwarts as Primo Carnera, Tony Galento and Tami Mauriello, we now had Rocco Marchegiano as the great Italian hopeful. And we got to see him up close and personal on TV as Rocky Marciano.

On the night of September 23, 1952, Rocky knocked Jersey Joe Walcott out cold with one short haymaker in the 13th round in Philadelphia to become the Heavyweight Champion of the World. As we cheered, I couldn't help but recall how Grandpop Lolli would have cherished the moment.

It is said that thousands of Italians, including hundreds in his hometown of Brockton, Massachusetts, bet the ranch on Rocky that night. The heroic accounts of the fight are legendary. Of how a smaller man with limited skills waded into the wheelhouse of a tough, hard-punching champion who was a master boxer, Fighting several rounds partially blinded by his own blood and medication, somehow surviving, and behind on points, he knocks out Walcottt with one short right. He goes on to be the only undefeated Heavyweight Champion in the annals of boxing.

On watching the films and reading the accounts, there is no doubt in my mind that Sylvester Stallone got his "Rocky" idea and script material from Marciano's career. Rocky is still Marciano and Marciano is Rocky. No doubt.

As a modern Italian teenager about to play high school football for Mt. St. Joe, I was very much into Rocky. Born September 1, 1923, in Brockton, Massachusetts, he was an American Legion Baseball catcher with a Major League dream. When he became a professional boxer, he wore the colors of Brockton High into the ring – a black robe with red letters. Always loyal to his roots, Rocky dedicated himself to the task of winning the title. He had great gifts: Stamina; a thick, rock-hard, compact body; the ability to absorb hard blows; and his own unorthodox overhand right, which he named "Suzy-Q." In addition, Rocky had an unusually thick bone structure around his chin and jaw. His handlers would tell Benny Trotta's boys that Rocky's jaw was indestructible because of the thickness of his bones. Silly theory? It was never proven wrong. Rocky was old-world from his immigrant family roots to his ultra conservative approach to business. He paid a terrible price to Al Weil, his manager and teacher, who taught him how to fight and in the process, took the lion's share of the purses. Marciano would fight seven title fights grossing a weak total of 1.5 million dollars.

Through his rise to the top, Rocky was always a target for nefarious underworld shenanigans. There were overtures to "throw fights." But one thing that Marciano valued over money was pride. Blinkey Palermo and Frankie Carbo were hardened types who Rocky's instincts told him to avoid. But he did hook up with a lesser god in the person of Benjamino Magliano, alias Benny Trotta. Trotta owned the Club Troc on the notorious Baltimore Block. On the second floor was a gym. A former pro boxer who won 17 out of 21 bouts, Benny became a fight promoter and manager.

In Trotta, Rocky found a true-blue guy. He was tired of the big-timers and phonies. Benny had all the right ingredients. Connected just well enough to put deals together as a match-maker and promoter, he was a warm presence and he was Italian. They hit it off from the first. Big-time friends and small-time partners.

Benny quit school in the fifth grade and matriculated to the University of Hard Knocks. Eventually, he became a fight manager. He handled Pete Galiano, Irish Billy Carrigan, Lou Transparenti, Nick Kirsch, Gary Garver, and title contenders Jimmy McCallister and Holly Mims. Trotta once recalled, "I never forgot when Mims fought Rocky Castellani in Cleveland. They had a convenient power failure when Holly was getting the best of him. A couple of years later I met the men who had Castellani, and after we broke bread, they said, "You're a different kind of guy than we thought. Had we known you then we would have let your fighter get a better break."

Once you got to know Benny, you liked him. He definite-ly had underworld connections. He had his promoter's license revoked and did some short time. Benny was always well groomed, personable and approachable. A soft touch for charities and hard luck stories. In the 40's and 50's he was in full bloom.

Despite all of Rocky's phenomenal success, he became more and more an Old World Italian, suspicious and guarded. Much like the immigrants who hid their money in the mattresses, Marciano trusted no one. Because of Weil's financial stranglehold, Rocky took on special appearances and exhibitions to make more money. Even after retiring undefeated (49-0 in 1955), he still barnstormed and hid his cash. Thus his need for a guy like Benny.

One night Benny brought his buddy Rocky down to the famous Surf Club in East Baltimore. The place was owned by Mimmi Lorenzo, an old crony of Uncle Arnold. In the days before TV took over, Sunday nights at the Surf was "where it was at." Hot music and hot women with Al "Madman" Baitch blowing the wildest sax on the East Coast. The place was always packed. Overseeing the rabid mob was a Baltimore-born tough guy and bouncer par excellence by the name of Bobby Pomerlane. Known to all the local mobsters simply as

Rocky in Little Italy... testing Maria's cuisine. Sitting on the left is Rocky's pal Benny Trotta and his kid brother Anthony.

"Rabbit," he was a longshoreman by trade. Never the bully or instigator of trouble, he was the walk softy, carry a big stick type. A look, a nod, or a glare is all it took to put any troublemakers in their place. The one cardinal rule was, coat and tie or no admittance. This included the King of England and Rabbit stood on the threshold to enforce it.

One warm night, the music stopped and a murmur enveloped the revelers. Standing in the doorway was Benny Trotta and his entourage. In their midst was none other than Rocky Marciano, the retired, undefeated Heavyweight Champion of the World. He was tan and dressed casually in sandals, white ducks and an open Hawaiian shirt. Pleasantries and Italian embraces were exchanged. Benny was in his glory, all smiles. Then there was a dead silence as Rabbit invoked the "coat and tie" rule. Trotta protested, sputtering threats and invectives. His followers stiffened as Rabbit stood his ground. The retired Heavyweight Champion of the World was about to be bounced out of the Surf. Then, as if by magic, one of Baltimore's finest bee-hived, gum chewing waitresses appeared. She handed Rocky a large khaki jacket and cotton tie from the Surf's coat room. Taking it all in, Rocky smiled and nodded in understanding, slipped on the jacket and with a sheepish grin tied the tie. The music started back up, Rocky love-tapped Rabbit on the shoulder as if to say, "good job." Benny's entourage slipped into the ballroom to tumultuous applause, and a giant sigh of relief. The Rabbit had held his ground and kept the integrity of the Surf Club and so did Rocky. But the very next day, Mimmi Lorenzo sent Rabbit down to Baltimore Street to deliver a personal apology to Benny.

Eventually, one of these "pick up some quick, tax free

cash" sorties cost Rocky his life. On August 31, 1969, at the young age of 46, his plane crashed in an Iowa cornfield. Rocky lived for the day and carried an indestructible persona within his heart. I think that he figured he could somehow walk away from a Cessna crash. Almost, but the tree he hit head on that day didn't budge. It was the only tree in the entire field. The night before Rocky and Benny were in Chicago and Benny turned down the opportunity to fly with Rocky to the Des Moines, Iowa event. It was said that much of Rocky's money was spread out to "dozens and dozens of friends and acquaintances" who cried, then breathed a sigh of relief when that plane crashed. Benny died two years later at the age of fifty-eight.

Two second generation Italian boys who became great friends for such a short time, they stayed loyal to their ethnic roots. What more can you ask.

Nick Mangione

"He was intrigued by the building trade as postwar America was rising upward in an unprecedented spiral. Nick went back to school to learn the rudiments of architecture and engineering. It was 1950 when his life began to turn."

Back at the turn of the 20th Century, Sicilian men would buy fruit and vegetables from boats docked at what is today's Baltimore Inner Harbor. Too poor to have carts or wagons, they loaded up their packs onto sagging shoulders and began their march up what is today Charles Street. Selling their wares along the way, moving ever northward toward the present day suburbs of Baltimore County, until they ran out of product.

A century later, following the same northern path, was another Sicilian who created a heavenly oasis in a land heretofore off limits to him and his people. Here is his story.

Every couple of months my dear friend Jim Hodges takes me to Hayfields for golf, good dining and great fellowship. Located just above the Baltimore Beltway in Hunt Valley, blue blood horse country. Due to Jim's unrelenting work schedule we play late in the day. The course is an immaculate emerald green oasis. And, when the sun sets in the west with the early harvest moon appearing over your left shoulder, you get a layman's look at what heaven could be like. I jokingly tell Jim that one late afternoon Jesus might descend from a nearby cloud to play nine. Who built this place anyway, and how did it mature so quickly? It's creator is Nick Mangione.

In 1945, at age 20, Nick Mangione of Baltimore, Maryland, circa Belair Market (the same neighborhood of the Vince Dundee-Lazzara family) was perched near the deck of the battleship Missouri in Tokyo Harbor. He got a bird's eye view of history, as he watched General MacArthur sign the Japanese surrender documents. This was heady stuff for a young kid barely out of his teens.

Returning home he began to take on America for size. Taking advantage of the G.I. Bill, he began to educate himself as a bookkeeper and accountant. He formed a strong understanding of what it takes to run a business. One of his clients was a contracting firm. He was intrigued by the building trade as postwar America was rising upward in an unprecedented spiral. Nick went back to school to learn the rudiments of architecture and engineering. It was 1950 when his life began to turn. First, he married Mary Cuba, a well educated and

The G.I. Bill of Rights Overpowers "La Via Vecchia"

As previously stated, over 1.5 million young Italian Americans fought for their country in World War II. On June 22, 1944, President Franklin D. Roosevelt signed the Servicemen's Readjustment Act of 1944, known as the G.I. Bill. A large percentage of these soldiers took advantage of the benefits to finance their higher education, take out loans for homes and business start-ups, as well as job searches and unemployment pay. These benefits placed Italian Americans directly in the mainstream of American life for the first time. After that, Italians swiftly became Americans and, also for the first time, tangibly separated themselves from the Old World ways of their parents and grandparents.

Rosemary M. Juras
Joseph M. Juras

Alexandra
Christina
Joseph

Louis Mangione
Kathleen (Zannino)

Maria Santa
Lucia
Luigi

John Mangione
Deborah (Pummery)

John Mario Jr.
Maria Delora
Victoria
Michael Robert

Linda M. Licata
Robert J. Licata

Stephen Nicholas
Victor Nicholas
Lisa Maria

Nick Mangione Jr.
Danielle (Toskes)

Nicholas III
Nino
Marco
Gianna (Gigi)
Phillip
Mia

Joanne M. Hock
John C. Hock

Nicole
Julianna
Johnna

Peter M. Mangione
Tracy (Dolan)

Nicholas
Joseph
Peter Dean

Frances M. O'Keefe
Gerard (Jerry) O'Keefe

Christine
Genevieve
Tommy
Celeste

Sam Mangione
Katie (Hart)

Mary Ellen
Julia Rose
Nicholas David
Luisa Maria
Peter Timothy

Michelle M. Collison
Keith H. Collison

Nicoletta

229

cultured young woman who was also the child of immigrants. Next, he formed Commercial Contractors, Inc. Both endeavors took off like a rocket.

Fourteen hour days were the norm. His family doctor said, "work eight and play six, get a hobby." Nick found golf. He took lessons and played with his affluent buddies. After a while the two activities merged as Nick bought Turf Valley Country Club and, over time, enlarged and converted the property into a 54-hole club with a large conference center component. This experience served as a springboard to the Hayfields project. Five years in the planning and construction, this project actually had its genesis close to a half century earlier.

In Hunt Valley there were legal obstacles and behind the scenes shenanigans to keep the Hayfields project out. Nick refused to cave in to political and landed aristocracy and created a most unique club that now numbers some of his former objectors. Like the Sicilian men who double timed it up Charles Street in the 1890's, hard work prevailed. Only in America can a former cement finisher become an avid golfer on a pristine golf course that he created from scratch in a formerly restricted area.

More importantly, Nick and Mary raised ten children and are the proud grandparents of thirty-six grand children. Their offsprings help run the family's business empire. Not bad for a kid who worked a full time job at age 12 to support his family after his father's passing.

After serving his country in World War II, Nick used the system to his advantage. He could be Exhibit A for the postwar success of the G.I. Bill. Today, Nick and Mary are heavily involved in the community, the arts, and philanthropic endeavors. They are always aware of their heritage.

The son of immigrant parents whose father died when he was a young child, Nick Mangione would be the first to tell you that he loves this country and that first and foremost he is an American, a true member of "La Famiglia Americana," in good standing.

Bishop Mugavero

"During his time, Bishop Mugavero gained a national reputation as a champion of the poor and an opponent of racism."

From 1968 to 1990 Francis J. Mugavero served as the Bishop of Brooklyn. He was the leader of 1.6 million Catholics. He passed away in 1991 at the age of 76.

Known for his humanity, he was a staunch advocate of human rights. He remembered his own early upbringing. Born of Sicilian immigrant parents, in the back of his father's barber shop in Bedford Stuyvesant on June 8, 1914, he was one of six children born to Angelo and Rose Mugavero.

Ordained in 1940 by Bishop Malloy, he rose to the position of Bishop for the Diocese of Brooklyn. The first Italian ever in a slot always reserved for the Irish. His distinguished career was earmarked by service to the poor and immigrant populations. He often called Brooklyn, "the diocese of immigrants." Mass was said in 17 different languages and in one school of 350, there were 28 ethnic backgrounds represented. He emphasized diversity and humanity for his priests, making every seminarian attend a language institute. The Bishop was always fond of "Brooklynese" and would always say to his striving parishioners, "You done good."

During his time, Bishop Mugavero gained a national

reputation as a champion of the poor and an opponent of racism. Under his leadership the Diocese became the major financial backer of the model Nehemiah Housing Program in East New York. He used Church facilities and properties to provide services to children in Headstart and Day Care programs and provided food programs for the hungry. He became the director of Catholic Charities in one of the most turbulent eras of American history, the decade of civil rights, the war on poverty, urban upheaval and the Vietnam War. During this period he was acclaimed, respected and bestowed many honors.

As a child he grew up in an upscale German/Irish neighborhood with families who had been around for decades. In those days Italians were the new kids on the block and lived in poor ghetto type conditions. The Mugaveros considered themselves lucky to be away from the

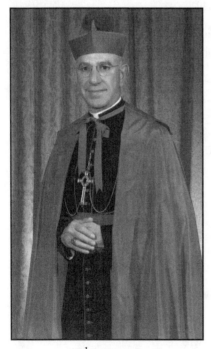
Bishop Mugavero

squalor despite having no support system. And, it is interesting to note that none of the Bishop's five siblings married an Italian. In a way this scenario is not far removed from my father's early flight from Little Italy. I'm sure that there is common blood there. The Mugaveros of Brooklyn and Baltimore's Little Italy were both from the tiny Sicilian village of Caltavuturo. The names are spelled the same and we look like him. And, my grandfather, Gregorio Mugavero, came over here and settled in New York. Though I tried to establish a blood connection, the assimilation process started in the 1920's rendered my efforts for naught. I received a cold shoulder from every call I made to a Mugavero in the Brooklyn phone directory. But, that's O.K. They are Siciliano and it's only 2002.

From the Bishop's bio came revelations I first heard from my father, that Sicilians had deep Spanish origins. In Caltavuturo, he was told by a priest, the Spanish pronunciation of Mugavero was with an "h" instead of a hard "g." Thus MooHAVero.

As the irony of the American Melting Pot unfolds, my first born son, Stephen, worked in New York for four years. He met and married Lucy Gonzales, a full blood-ed Spanish girl. And, on September 13, 2002, they welcomed their first child, Austin Luis Baker. Sicilian and Spanish, he will truly belong to La Famiglia Americana. And, the Bishop of Brooklyn from Caltavuturo would be

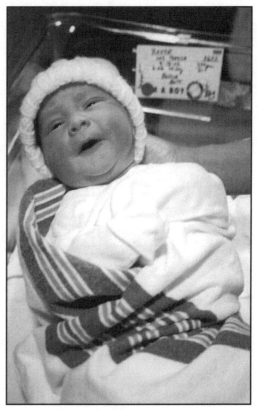

The 5th Generation
Austin Luis Baker

very pleased.